RETURN TO
PATTON'S
FRANCE

By the Same Author

1996: D'UTAH BEACH AUX ARDENNES, ITINERAIRES 1944–1994. Vendôme, France: Presses Universitaires de France, A Horizons for Learning Publication. Retracing the World War II itinerary of the author with Patton's Third Army.

1994: TANGIER AND ALL THAT, a historico-literary study of American, British and French writers and artists living or working in Tangier, Morocco, focusing on the post-World War II era. Three Continents Press, Colorado Springs, Colorado.

1994: SHATTERED VISION, a translation of Rabah Belamri's *Regard blessé*, Holmes and Meier Publishers, New York, New York.

1993: REMEMBRANCE OF A TIME JUST PAST, an English version of Guillermo's Arango's (a bilingual edition) of *Memoria de un pasado inmediato*. New Jersey: Linden Lane Press.

1990: STAGING A SPANISH CLASSIC: THE HOUSE OF FOOLS, including a bilingual edition of Valdivielso's HOSPITAL DE LOS LOCOS, with Dr. John D. Mitchell. The Northwood Institute Press, Midland, Michigan.

1990: THE DISTANT FRIEND, a translation of Claude Roy's *L'ami lointain*, Holmes and Meier, New York, New York.

1990: THE SIMPLE PAST, a translation of Driss Chraibi's *Le passé simple*, Three Continents Press, Washington, D.C.

1990: "Gertrudis Gómez de Avellaneda," in SPANISH AMERICAN WOMEN WRITERS, A BIOGRAPHICAL SOURCE BOOK, Greenwood Press, Westport, Connecticut.

1989: MOTHER SPRING, a translation of Driss Chraibi's *La mère du printemps*, Three Continents Press, Washington, D.C.

1987: SHADOW OF PARADISE, bilingual edition of Nobel Laureate Vicente Aleixandre's *Sombra del Paraíso*, The University of California Press, Berkeley, California. Paperback edition, 1992.

1983: MOTHER COMES OF AGE, a translation with introduction of Moroccan author Driss Chraibi's *La civilization, ma mère!...*, Three Continents Press, Washington, D.C.

1982: THE BUTTS, a translation with introduction of Driss Chraibi's *Les boucs*, Three Continents Press.

1981: GERTRUDIS GOMEZ DE AVELLANEDA, a biography and critical study of the Cuban-born nineteenth-century author, The Twayne Series, D.C. Hall, Boston, Massachusetts.

1977: FEMMES/HOMBRES, a bilingual edition with introduction, with Messrs. Mitchell and Packard, of Paul Verlaine's work, The Chicago Review Press, Chicago, Illinois. Paperback edition: New York, IASTA Publications, 1992.

1971: A HISTORY OF SPANISH LITERATURE (reissued in 1981), a translation with an English Preface, Introduction, Introductory Chapter, and Addendum, of Guillermo Díaz-Plaja's *Historia de la literatura española*, New York University Press, New York, New York.

1963: A SECOND SPANISH HANDBOOK FOR TEACHERS IN ELEMENTARY SCHOOLS, with R.C. Allen, Jr., the University of Pittsburgh, Pittsburgh, Pennsylvania.

1962: THE SCAVENGER, a translation with introduction of Francisco de Quevedo's *Vida del Buscón*, Las Américas Publishing Company, New York, New York.

1961: A FIRST SPANISH HANDBOOK FOR TEACHERS IN ELEMENTARY SCHOOLS, with R.C. Allen, Jr., The University of Pittsburgh Press.

1960: RINCONETE Y CORTADILLO, with Willis Barnstone, a text edition of Miguel de Cervantes' picaresque novel, Las Américas Publishing Company, New York, New York.

Cover: Vendôme, Place Saint-Martin, 18 August 1944

RETURN TO PATTON'S FRANCE

1944s Odyssey retraced

HUGH A. HARTER

With a preface by Helen Patton-Plusczyk

JANUS PUBLISHING COMPANY
London, England

First published in Great Britain 1999
by Janus Publishing Company Limited,
Edinburgh House, 19 Nassau Street,
London W1N 7RE

www.januspublishing.co.uk

A CIP catalogue record for this book
is available from the British Library.

ISBN 1 85756 445 6

Phototypeset in 12 on 15 Sabon
by Keyboard Services, Luton, Beds

Cover design John Anastasio, Creative Line

Printed and bound in Great Britain by
Athenaeum Press Ltd, Gateshead, Tyne & Wear

For Frannie, for the past,
the present, and whatever the future
may bring.

CONTENTS

PREFACE

Helen Ayer Patton

"If you build on it, they will come."

from the film *A Field of Dreams*

I met Hugh and Frances Harter on D-9, 1994, in the village of Néhou which is dead center of the Cotentin Peninsula, twenty-five minutes from every coast, nestled between a maze of snarled hedgerows, and concealed like a well-covered baby chick. My grandfather was a great believer that one look is worth a thousand maps, but anyone hoping to pinpoint the exact place where Patton and the 365 men of his Command staff sequestered themselves for a month prior to the breakout at Avranches, needs a good "army" map.

This initiative came from the nuns of the Abbey of Regina Laudis in Bethlehem, Connecticut and their Abbess, Mother Benedict Duss. She had been a novice at Notre Dame de Juarre just east of Paris during five years of German Occupation, and on August 27th Juarre was liberated by a faction of the Third Army headed in the direction of Reims. She spotted a five-pointed star on one of the tanks and which was her first glimpse of a war that she had felt but had not seen. In the same moment, Mother Benedict was inspired to return to her native America and found a Benedictine Abbey in the French tradition and committed to the life of prayer founded on gratitude for the Liberation by Allied Forces.

Fifty years later, Lady Abbess and my sister Margaret Georgina Patton, who had since joined the Benedictine order in Connecticut, began to pursue the exact whereabouts of the Néhou orchards. They were driven by the knowledge that matter never forgets and that the orchards would remember. It was important to return to the orchard where Patton and his men had been forced into a kind of contemplative (cloistered) existence prior to embarking on what would henceforth come to be known as "La Voie de la Liberté" (The Road of Liberty); if the orchard could in some way be held and cared for by the nuns in prayer and in memory of all those called to pour themselves into the fight for freedom, it would stand as a still point forever present in the center of the chaos and destruction that had been World War II.

Letters verifying the location of the orchard were sent by Lt. General Orwin Talbot, my father, Major General George S. Patton IV, and Cpt. Allison Wysong who had been by my grandfather's side from England to Czechoslovakia. These letters matched the evidence provided by WWII historian Henri Levaufre and Mr. Jean Tyson. Tyson was twenty when he was given a secret pass into the CP's medical unit. His baby sister was having her teeth fixed by one of the military dentists. While in the waiting area, Jean encountered "a man much older than the rest, who seemed in charge of everything. He was limping." (Patton had broken his toe!) This meeting made such an impression on Jean that he became a secret guardian to the orchard and its memory. He was scrutinized and criticized for his tireless homage to these Americans, who as far as many of his peers were concerned had come and gone like fair-weather friends. But the fool became the wise man, and Jean was vindicated when at last the facts were gathered and the Département of La Manche purchased the orchard, retaining three acres for the display of a monument, a Sherman tank (provided by the Military Academy of Saumur). The other three acres were entrusted to the Lady Abbess and the community of Regina Laudis.

I lived alone in Néhou in an abandoned 17th-century priory for monks, and worked daily with Mr. Tyson and the mayor of Néhou, Mr. Le Chevalier, for a period of eleven months. Only one of the apple trees that had stood in the orchard in 1944 remained, and that one still stands at the center of the 363 baby trees that we planted in 1993. The first apple appeared on the very spot where Mr. Tyson and Grandpa met. I knew he would be thrilled that after a long search, I found and sent to him a photo of Grandpa in the field appearing just as he would have remembered. Once and for all, he would have proof positive that it was indeed "Patton" that he had seen.

I cannot explain why Jean Baptiste Tyson died unexpectedly only minutes before the photo arrived. Nor can I explain why my other right-hand man, Mr. Jean Le Chevalier, was killed in a car accident on May 9th, 1994. Just days before, we had placed a 3000 pound bolder in the field, and had inscribed on it two phrases that were repeated over and over by Patton during the war: "Do not take counsel of your fears" and the battle cry he borrowed from Danton: "De L'audace! Encore de L'audace! Toujours de L'audace!"

Both Jean Baptiste and Jean lived for the fiftieth anniversary of the Allied landings and the return of the American soldiers. On June 11th 1994, 1500 people came from all over the world to participate in the Dedication of the Néhou Orchard and "Camp Patton." My faith being the size of mustard seed, I do believe these two men had the best view of the parade. Someone said that the reason Patton himself had been taken away so abruptly was that the men who had died needed their leader with them. If so, perhaps the two Jeans were also needed, and perhaps they were instrumental in leading Hugh Harter to Néhou.

According to the 148th Psalm, we souls are given tasks that never change. Those who have crossed over continue from elsewhere. My task is just now being determined. Hugh was the very first Veteran to return to the Néhou orchard, and brought with him the glorious gift of continuity between what happened, what is happening now, and what can happen if we honor our "task," by living into our call. This is precisely what is unique and at the heart of this book. Hugh is a soldier, an educator, a poet, and most importantly, a dreamer. His dedication to the arts has been a great inspiration to me as I work to build a theater in Néhou. On land held in perpetuity by an abbey that was born out of war, we are driven to help launch the next fifty years by producing theatrical works that commemorate freedom, and forge to the depths of what it means to live it and keep it. As you experience through Hugh being whisked across France with Patton's Third in 1944 and then retrace the threads in 1994, bear in mind the memory of the future.

ACKNOWLEDGEMENTS

THIS TALE OF two epochs, 1944 and the 1990s, owes a debt to many friends on both sides of the Atlantic. Some of them have been from the war period. Others have become friends more recently. Their stories of the war, the Occupation of France, the Resistance, and so on, have become interwoven with my own. These men and women have greatly aided in the remembering of a time long past, but still incredibly vivid in memory. The reader will meet many of them here.

First of all, there has been the hard work and efforts of my dear friend Christian Couppé of Blois, without whose help this book could not have taken shape. Christian phoned, wrote letters, sent faxes, checked phone numbers on the family Minitel, and was the invaluable sleuth who ferreted out the people of half a century ago on my first "trek" across France, all expenses paid by Uncle Sam. Christian has been a World War II buff since the age of seven when he witnessed the American bombing of a railway bridge across the Loire River near Blois. He was at his grandfather's home in a small village where part of the family still resides. The bridge has not been rebuilt, but for Christian its memory has stayed alive and given birth to a large collection of war souvenirs and a library that overflows enticingly throughout the house onto steps and into cellar and attic. He nurtured and abetted the writing of this book, as did his wife Christiane who took us in, fed us and cared for us with affection and deliciously fattening food, and who died so tragically in an accident. First thanks, therefore, to the Couppé family for all they have done, and to the memory of Christiane.

There are others in Blois who have also been singularly helpful. Dr. Raymond Jacob and his wife Jeanne (Janou) have gone out of their way to welcome us and to help in my search for people and their histories. Janou is President of the Loir et Cher chapter of the Societé France-USA, a society of friendship between our two countries that has been greatly aided and fostered by Janou's sagacious leadership.

At the same time that I first met the Couppés and the Jacobs, I was introduced to Raymond Casas, a veteran of the Resistance, author of three books on the war, raconteur and historian of the events of the Blois area during the war with a phenomenal memory and knowledge. He too has been of great help.

One person I really met in Blois on the night of 16 August 1944 was Jean Deck. After ceremonies in Blois on 17 August 1992, a stranger came up to me, told me his name, shook my hand, and said simply: "J'étais là." "I was there." Further contact revealed that Jean Deck was a young Resistance fighter who still vividly remembers his astonishment at meeting four American non-coms the night of 16 August who had shown up in two jeeps. His story is an exciting one of courage and integrity. I am proud to say that we are now close friends. Two years later on, we found the Resistance fighter who had been on the terrace of the chateau of Blois, Georges Fabre who told me it was the late Charles "Charlot" Hervé who had saved my life that night.

Other new friends have facilitated and helped: Jim Lemire, an American veteran now deceased, who returned to France to marry his lovely sweetheart, Marie Louise Lemire, herself a decorated member of the Resistance, former president of the SAR in France. Count Michel and Countess de Rochambeau, Viscount Hubert Jurien de la Gravière of Vendôme, Nicole Blu and her brother Guy Chenais of Le Mans. From eastern France: good friend and Resistance member Hubert Payon, along with his brother, the Abbot, now both deceased, and his wife Mimi from Nancy. Michel Hachet of the Municipal Museum of Toul, dear friends Maryse Audoyer Verpeau, now of Aix-en-Provence, and Emile (Mimi), recently deceased and Paule Gallien, of Laxou (Nancy), warm and welcoming throughout the years.

Special thanks also for the sharing of the extraordinary gouaches of Claude Rémusat (1896–1981), artistic adviser to the Bibliotheque Nationale in Paris and veteran of the First World War and Resistance fighter in the Second. The fascinating paintings of life for us GIs in the southern Normandy Cotentin Peninsula in August and September 1944 provide a new and singular visual record of what those of us in Third Army lived through in our orchard "homes" at that time. Jean-Luc Leservoisier of the Musée Municipal d'Avranches has magnanimously given permission to use one of them for this volume and for other publications in the future.

In the Dombasle area, Couppé and I were warmly greeted and shown around by a group of former members of the Resistance: Pierre Ballé, Jean Césard, Raymond Grimm, René Fresse, and co-hosts Claude Wrobel, Gérard Berge, Michel Caps, and Mayor Robert Blaise. In 1994, I re-found friend Odette Schneider, since deceased, who laughingly recalled how I bounded energetically up the stairs to my Solvay office.

Among those persons rediscovered, in addition to Hubert Payon, is René Marin, now of Paris, but living in Sens when we became friends, whose lovely wife Odette has been as helpful as René in providing information on the liberation of Sens. His daughter, Isabelle, as I mention, is a close school friend of Anne Charlotte Bougenaux, daughter of Paul Bougenaux, one of my closest friends for many years before his death.

On the American side, telephone information operators here in the States helped relocate highly decorated (including the French Legion of Honor) former Lieutenant Colonel Roland H. Breton, the commanding officer of my MI Team #443 during the four campaigns we participated in, Normandy, Northern France, Rhineland, and Ardennes, and CIC member Ralph Palmer, in the same campaigns with us who went on with Third Army into Germany in 1945. Both Roland and Ralph furnished invaluable information and photographs of our shared experience in France.

No acknowledgements could be complete without thanks to the Lenoir family, which took me in as one of their own. Our mutual attachment to "Papou" Fernand Lenoir, and "Mamie" Elisa Delambre Lenoir lasted until their deaths, and now goes on through Pierre, wife Hélène, and their children.

A recent trip to England made a visit to Peover Hall a

possibility. We were guests in the small town of Knutsford where Patton lived for most of the six months before going into Normandy. Many thanks for the hospitality of Mayor and Mayoress Derek Squirell, the Vicar, Reverend Kenneth Burghall and wife Maureen, Jennifer Holbrook, former mayoress, Member of Parliament Martin Bell, and especially to Kenneth Oultram who did the arrangements for the annual Patton luncheon in Knutsford. Present owner of Peover Hall, Mr. Randle Brooks, graciously invited us into the Hall to see the great room where Patton entertained.

The excitement of meeting Patton's two granddaughters, Mother Margaret Georgina at La Flamme Vivante and her sister Helen Ayer Patton in Néhou, has continued in a growing friendship with Helen and participation in her burgeoning plans to make Néhou something of a center for study of the war and efforts for peace and reconciliation. I have also had the honor and the pleasure of meeting General George S. Patton IV and his charming wife Joanne, sons George, Robert and Benjamin Patton. Robert's excellent book on the family, *The Pattons*, is a must reader for anyone interested in "Georgie", and those before and after him.

Sincere thanks to Helen for her excellent preface and her loving friendship. Patton now has a new great-grandson, Ingmar, son of Helen and husband Dr. Thorsten Plusczyk.

Editorial suggestions from Katharine Turok Goldberger, from my stepdaughter, Ellen Uma Berliner, and from Rebecca Lewis of Barcelona, have been of great importance as well. Thanks also to Wesley Bennett for work on the photographs.

Last, but certainly, not least, is my gratitude, as always, to my wife Frances who cares for me as well as the manuscripts as they come through the computer. She has a sharply perceptive eye, a sensitive tongue, and a loving heart which shapes the manuscript, warms the spirit, and nourishes the man. Never much of a war buff until we got into the reading and visits preparatory to the writing of this book, she now has become almost as involved and interested in matters of World War II as myself, but remains, as do I, a dedicated lover of peace. And to my mother, who lived through both World Wars, and who has always been a fighter herself in the best sense of the word.

New York, 1998

PERMISSIONS

The obtaining of permissions to quote from works published since the war has been greatly complicated by several factors. Many publishers in the years immediately after the war no longer exist or have been absorbed into the huge conglomerates that dominate publishing in America today. Some of the military books were printed by small companies impossible to trace. Such is the case of the extremely rare book on XII Corps written and/or edited by Lt. Col. George Byer and printed in Baton Rouge, Louisiana (where coincidentally, I had been sent for some special training in 1943). There is no trace of the publishing company, and consequently no permissions could be obtained. The same is true for Brenton G. Wallace's book on Patton and the Third Army, published in 1946 by the Military Service Publishing Company in Harrisburg and Washington D.C.

The Vanguard Press that did Robert S. Allen's *Lucky Forward* has apparently been swallowed up by a conglomerate. I was unable to find to whom I should address a request for permission. This is also the case for Ladislas Ferago's excellent biography of Patton, first copyrighted by Faracorn Ltd., and then to Ivan Obulensky of New York. Oscar W. Koch's book on Intelligence for Third Army was published by the Whitmore Publishing Company in Philadelphia, now no longer listed in phone or publishing manuals.

COMBAT CHRONOLOGY

XII Corps sailed from New York on 9 April 1944 arriving in Greenock on 16 April. Corps landed on 17 April and went by rail directly to Stourport, its first camp, where it arrived on 18 April. Corps' second camp was at Birmingham (15 June). From Birmingham Corps moved through Oxford, Swindon, and Salisbury, arriving at its third camp, Braemore, on 9 July. The night of 24 July was spent in an assembly area at Camp Hursley, near Southampton. Embarkation took place 25 July.

XII Corps landed in France 27 July at Utah Beach, just N of Carentan, and bivouacked near there for the night. The next day Corps moved to a bivouac area near Bricquebec (Quettetot).

Sartilly (6–14 August). XII Corps became operational 12 August when Maj Gen Gilbert R Cook received the following order from Gen Patton: "XII Corps will concentrate SE of Le Mans, prepared to operate to N, NE, or E, protect S flank of Army." The order might have added, "and the right flank of the entire AEF."

Le Mans (14–17 August). On 14 August Corps' CP was set up at Le Mans; its immediate objective was Orleans. By 17 August Orleans and Chateaudun had been cleared.

Fontaine (17–21 August). 17 August Maj Gen Gilbert R Cook gave up his command because of ill health. Maj Gen John S Wood was acting commander 17–19 August, when Maj Gen Manton S. Eddy assumed command.

Chevilly (21–23 August). XII Corps seized bridgeheads over the Yonne River at Sens (21 August) and over the Loing River at Souppes (22 August). Montargis was captured.

Mignerette (23–24 August). Progress was so rapid that the CP stayed in this suburb of Montargis only one day.

Sens (24–28 August). On 26 August Corps seized a bridgehead over the Seine and captured Troyes.

Villadin (28–31 August). Chalons was captured and bridgeheads established over the Marne and Aube Rivers (29 August). By 30 August Corps had covered 250 miles in 16 days; gasoline supplies were critically low. The capture of 155,000 gallons at Chalons and Blesme enabled the advance to continue.

Sompuis (31 August–4 September). By now well versed in amphibious operations, Corps seized bridgeheads beyond the Meuse and Ornain rivers and captured Commercy (31 August). 116,000 gallons of gasoline were captured near Commercy.

Guerpont (4–9 September). Beginning 5 September American troops attempted to force the Moselle River. Only XII Corps succeeded.

Foug (9–18 September). By the middle of September XII Corps had forged a giant bridgehead across the Moselle. The Meurthe River was crossed 13 September. On the 15th Nancy was captured and Le Sanon River crossed.

Nancy (18 September–8 November). At the beginning of the period Corps crossed the Marneau-Rhin Canal and established a bridgehead over the Seine river. Restraining line was set up 23 September. During October Corps maintained and improved its positions along this line and repulsed heavy enemy counterattacks. Dieuze Dam was bombed 20 October to prevent Germans from flooding the Seine while Corps was expanding its bridgehead.

Essey-les-Nancy (8–14 November). XII Corps launched attack on Maginot Line, which Germans had rebuilt and reoriented. Chateau Salins was captured 10 November.

Chateau Salins (14–23 November). Corps troops captured intact a bridge over the Nied Allemande River.

Morhange (23 November–8 December). For its part in the capture of Metz (24 November) XII Corps was specially commended by both Gen Marshall and Gen Patton. By 25 November Corps had smashed the Maginot Line. The Maderbach and Eichel Rivers were crossed (4 December). 279 towns and villages were liberated during November.

Sarralbe (8–21 December). In spite of floods, mud, and heavy opposition, Corps forced a crossing of the Blies River into Germany (12 December). Sarreguemines was cleared (11 December).

Luxembourg (21 December–24 February). In 4 days and 5 nights Corps moved from Saar Region to Luxembourg (80,000 men and 11,000 vehicles) and halted the German breakthrough N of Luxembourg City. By year's end Corps' mission of seizing and holding the Sauer Moselle Line was accomplished. By end of January enemy was thrust back into Germany. 7 February attacked across swift, flooded Sauer and Our rivers into heart of Siegfried Line. By 10 February the Siegfried Line was smashed. 23 February units reached Prum River.

Fels (24 February–4 March). Corps forced the Nims River on 24 February, the Prum River on 26 February, and the Kyll River on 3 March – all three were flooded at time of crossing. On 28 February the important road center of Bitburg was captured.

Echternach (4–8 March). After a swift advance Corps units on 7 March reached the heights of E Saffig overlooking the Rhine River.

Bitburg (8–12 March). On 8 March Koblenz, at the junction of the Rhine and Moselle rivers, was pocketed.

Mayen (12–19 March). On 14 March Corps forced a crossing of the Moselle in the Hatzenport-Treis area, a move which threw the enemy off balance and resulted in the destruction of most of his forces in the Moselle-Saar triangle. Corps again crossed the Moselle to Bullay (17 March) and the Nahe River (17 March).

Simmern (19–22 March). Corps captured Mainz and Worms (21 March).

Bad Kreuznach (22–27 March). First assault crossing of the Rhine in history was made by XII Corps at Oppenheim on 22 March. By 24 March two bridges had been built and the bridgehead was secure. 25 March Darmstadt was captured and the bridges across the Main at Hanau and Aschaffenburg seized.

Gross Gorau (27–30 March). The area from Frankfurt to Hanau was cleared. Corps units advanced 35 miles N of the Main.

Offenbach (30 March—3 April). In half a month Corps had crossed the Moselle, Rhine, and Main Rivers. In one month it had advanced 215 miles and captured 67,000 prisoners.

Lauterbach (3–6 April). With the capture of Suhl Corps was within 65 miles of Czechoslovakia. Gotha was taken.

Vacha (6–9 April). At Merkers Salt Mine Corps uncovered Reichsbank Gold Reserve (estimated at 100 tons) along with huge quantities of silver, paper currency, objets d'art, and valuable paintings stolen from all over Europe.

Meiningen (9–13 April). Here Corps captured

the entire German prisoners of war files. On 12 April Corps captured Coburg and Eisfeld.

Eisfeld (13–15 April). Corps advanced rapidly to the SE, capturing Kronach (13 April) and Bayreuth (14 April).

Kronach (15–21 April). On 18 April Corps cut Germany in two by crossing into Czechoslovakia. On 20 April Gen Eddy relinquished his command because of ill health and was replaced by Maj Gen S Le Roy Irwin.

Bayreuth (21–24 April). Corps captured Asch (21 April), first large Czech town entered by American troops. Other units pushed rapidly SE toward the Austrian border.

Garfenwöhr (24–26 April). Here Corps discovered a huge dump containing approximately 2,000,000 poison gas shells.

Schwarzenfeld (26–29 April). On 26 April Corps units crossed into Austria – the first American troops to do so.

Viechtach (29 April–3 May). Of the 6,000 who died on the Flossenberg death march, 204 were murdered at Neunberg. On 29 April, under Corps auspices, a funeral was held for them attended by the entire population of the town.

Grafenau (3–28 May). XII Corps celebrated VE-Day at Grafenau. Among Corps' achievements during the last days of the war were its capture of Linz and the deepest penetration of Czechoslovakia. Mauthausen, biggest of the death camps, where an average of 250 a day were killed, was liberated. On 9 May near Strenburg, Corps made the first linkup between American and Russian forces in Austria.

I

AS OUR TWO jeeps drove into the city of Blois that late afternoon, the only signs of life were tracer bullets shining against a darkening sky. The streets were empty, not a living soul in sight. I was riding shotgun in the second jeep, two collaborators in the first jeep and one in the front seat of the second. Two men and a woman. We didn't know if they were dangerous or not. They certainly seemed like just ordinary people caught up in the muddle of occupation and war, but we had been warned not to take any chances. They were from Blois, but offered no comment or guidance as we followed the street in the direction of what we supposed to be the center, the center over which the bullets had been making a halo.

Blois is at the head of the chateau country of France, that area the French call *la douce France*, the France of gentle breezes and softly rolling countryside. It is there that the sweetness of the climate and the landscape blends with the soil to produce a bounty of food and wines, and where small rivers delight the eye as fully as the cuisine delights the palate. It had the reputation of a pastoral Eden dotted with fairytale castles.

The France where we found ourselves in that August of 1944, however, was anything but a haven of peace and bucolic tranquility. It was a cauldron of struggle and turmoil as the Allied forces began exploiting the famous breakthrough. Patton's Third Army had initiated it at the end of July at the southern tip of Normandy at Avranches. In most of the countryside and villages we passed through, the population gave us a tumultuous welcome, but we knew that not everyone was for us. There were those who collaborated with the Germans, those who had been a part of the Vichy regime of Marshal Pétain and his sinister henchman, Pierre Laval. There was a nucleus of people who had vested interests to protect. They wanted a German victory, not an Allied one. It was a part of our job to ferret out the collaborationists to prevent their giving any help to the enemy and to protect our troops from attempted sabotage by the forces that still numbered in the tens of thousands as we moved deeper into France.

We were aware of all of that in Blois as our jeeps kept on driving down the abandoned street. Where, we wondered, were the other Americans? Why were there no Resistance fighters to meet us, no people waving home-made American flags, tossing us flowers or holding out a glass of wine? What was happening in this silent and seemingly deserted city? After all, in Normandy, despite the desecration and ruin of towns and cities, the French greeted us like victors, the conquerors of the evil forces they had suffered under for four long years. Some minutes later, we had answers to our questions. We had come to the town's center.

The great chateau of Blois looms high over the very heart of the city. Our jeeps rounded a curve, and suddenly there before us it stood, so startling in its beauty and its splendor that for a moment we almost forgot the mission that had brought us here: to turn the collaborators over to the American military authorities or to the French. Why had they been sent to Vendôme to us in the first place, the major had asked earlier that afternoon, but no one could answer that. A little truck run on ersatz fuel had deposited them with us and driven off. South it went over the old stone bridge across from the small hotel where we had set up what could be called "regional intelligence headquarters" two days earlier. Beside the bridge was, and is, a sign and an arrow pointing to Blois. We knew nothing about Blois, I must admit, but did take the trouble to find out that it was about 19 miles away, a short drive on a warm summer's afternoon.

There were four of us, Earl Coon, master sergeant of Military Intelligence team 443 to which I belonged, and two Counter Intelligence agents, named, if memory serves, Bud Hock and Gale Hart. Coon and I spoke French, the CIC men did not. All four of us knew that this was chateau country, but none of us had anticipated anything as spectacular as this. A real movie set! We pulled up to the dual staircase that led up to the areaway ringing the building. I jumped out of the jeep, told my comrades I would find out what was going on, and trotted jauntily up the steps.

Up above was the vast terrace of the castle. Not too far from me, I saw a Frenchman. He was crouching at the other side of an opening. As it was described to me years later, I "bounded" across the areaway toward him to ask what was happening. The man rushed forward, grabbed me and threw me down. "Are you trying to get yourself killed?" he growled in French. To him I owed my life, as the Germans were actively peppering the area with mortar shells and machine-gun bullets.

Half a century later, my recollection of the event was

3

corroborated. I also learned the name of my benefactor. It was Charles Hervé, now deceased, whom his comrades nicknamed Charlot or Charlie. He was a member of a team of six Resistance fighters assigned earlier that afternoon to defend the terrace of the chateau under active fire from the Germans. It was only a couple of hours earlier that the enemy had withdrawn to the other side of the Loire River after duly blowing up the center of the massive stone bridge that was the city's main crossing point.

Whether Charlot was the first to ask "But where are the Americans?" or whether it was I, I can no longer remember. It was certainly the beginning of our conversation, one that became rather heated as other members of the group angrily insisted that we Americans had let the Resistance down. The French FFI themselves had liberated the town that very afternoon. Now they were fearful of a massive German counter-attack across a knee-deep river that could have easily been forded in large numbers. It was a Hollywood plot with a Hollywood setting, complete with dark cellars lit only by flickering candles set into old wine bottles. We all felt a sense of deepening urgency born out of apprehension for these new comrades and for the defenseless townspeople barricaded in their houses.

It was August 16th. My three GI comrades and I had "liberated" Blois, or at least could be considered part of it, the American part of it! For years, however, our arrival went untold and unnoticed. The histories of the liberation of Blois declared that a jeep arrived the morning of the 17th with the first Americans. Not so. That jeep had come the night before. Coon and one of the CIC men stayed on at a downtown hotel, probably the former Kommandantur, while the other CIC comrade and I hastened back through

4

a moonless night to report to headquarters what was going on down by the Loire.

I first told that part of my story to a rather astonished matron, patroness of a charming bed-and-breakfast on the banks of the River Loire in 1991. She promptly got in touch with friends who knew people who had been part of the Resistance in 1944. That very day, the plot took on new depth and unsuspected turns and twists for me. The war was long behind me, but its truth came marching on, with a clarion call to find out more about the past I had somehow tried to bury. How accurate was my memory? Who would help me find that past and unravel it? I soon found out.

Three people came to see me at the bed-and-breakfast: the president of the local chapter of the society of US-French friendship, Madame Janette Jacob, a man asking me to do a radio broadcast the next day, and a World War II buff, Christian Couppé, soon to become one of my closest friends. The ball was rolling after forty-seven years. I was interviewed on radio and for the local newspaper with local WWII historian and Resistance fighter Raymond Casas. The next year, Fran and I were invited back. The story, in many ways had just begun. The initial challenge was to find out more about that night of August 16th, and as that plot began its twists and turns and revelations, others took form. That marvelous French invention of the Minitel made it possible to rediscover former friends all over northern France. Old friends were still alive, and new ones sprang into the breaches, each with stories of heroism and heartbreak, still vividly recalled half a century later. They helped stitch together that experience, never forgotten but seldom mentioned, of being part of an incredible historic moment in an army and under a commander whose fame has become legendary.

I spent a great deal of time in France in the intervening years, much of it in Paris with close French friends, but as the half-century date began to loom ever larger on the calendar, I kept saying that I wanted to go back to Utah Beach once more, both to Normandy and beyond. It was almost by accident at the bed-and-breakfast on the Loire that fate impelled me into the world I had been a part of so long ago. My story was of interest, in France, at least. The time had come to remember rather than to forget.

Some photographs taken by French families, sent home for me in 1944, and a shabby address book provided key links to the past. New friends and old, from Blois, Vendôme, Avranches, Sens and Lorraine helped me sift through the past. They asked me questions, and at times I found myself reverting to the role of interrogator. Often I could not answer either my friends' or my own questions to my satisfaction. It became a kind of obligation to enlighten myself in order to enlighten others. I found some exciting reading on those musty library shelves and added to my growing collection of war literature.

First I had to confront some questions. Fortunately there were answers, and some astonishing ones. The French have deified Patton and complain that they know little about him. I too found that I knew embarrassingly little about the commander under whom I had served. What was General George S. Patton Jr. really like, that complex and controversial figure who is the object of such veneration to this day? That was the historical level.

On the personal level, what had happened to the French people in my fading photos? Were they still alive? Could they be found again? Would they want to see me, to get to know me after all these years? I was risking disappointment, but at the same time, I was betting on the sense of loyalty and friendship of the French people to lend a hand in my search.

I was right. My instincts proved valid. Some of Patton's luck must have rubbed off on me! The time to re-examine what had happened in 1944 had indeed come. I was to relive my story in the France I had known and loved, an almost miraculous resuscitation through the stories of the men and women I knew in 1944 or have grown to know now. The dignity with which these men and women cloak their heroism is a lesson of modesty and taste. They have shared their moments of fear and courage with me, usually at my urging, and their tales and mine have built a picture of the path XII Corps Third Army took across France from Utah Beach in Normandy to the gates of Hitler's Third Reich.

The story of Third Army is too full to be casually put aside. In 1944, as a speaker of French I had an entrée that most of my fellow soldiers did not. It also gave me the privilege of tracking Patton's army fifty years later. During the war my mission was to question and pass on the information I obtained. Interestingly enough, I seem to be back at my old job, but this time out of uniform. Third Army's exploits in the war were and are high drama. My role in them was modest, but the story I tell is none the less moving.

II

I T MAY JUST be human nature to talk about
the good old days, but a lot of us veterans
talked little, if at all, about the war. No one
back home seemed interested. Getting back to normal as
quickly as possible dominated everybody's thoughts. It
wasn't that we forgot. We just shut up and tried to find
our way in a new world partly of our creation. Talking
about the war brought up painful memories and bored our
non-veteran friends. If we told anything, we jollied about
it, exaggerating the good times, having a laugh at this or
that supposed event, boasting of how we charmed the
ladies of France or England.

The America we had left was not the America we came
home to. What we had seen had changed us. Folks at home
seemed different too. Our experiences had separated us
from them, sometimes overtly and sometimes in subtle
ways. What our family and friends had *not* seen changed
them for *us*.

Often it seemed that people in the US were living in a
cocoon, unable or unwilling to recognize what had happened in the world beyond their garden gates. Having seen
a world with no moral strictures of any kind, where
human life had been stripped of value, it was hard to come
back to a myopic society with all its stigmas, where

attitudes towards race, religion, gender, and sex were set in concrete. For years, we had listened to that society's catchwords, Freedom, Honor, Sacrifice, and Truth. In those days non-conformity was sinful; most of us firmly believed in sin, and that resulted in a lot of sweeping under the rug. Internationally, we were Babes in the Wood, innocent and smug in our insularity.

It took Pearl Harbor to start the process of change. The results? A better America? A worse America? A matter very much up for grabs as we near the century's end. We may be a bit more tolerant to minorities, and we are surely more aware of what is happening in the world. We have learned a lot of geography.

The first lesson was on Hawaii. We suddenly found out that there was more to that Pacific Eden than the beach at Waikiki. That was on a Sunday, December 7th, 1941. We also learned that the Japanese could build warships, planes, torpedoes, and bombs. Our innocence was at an end. We had been deflowered.

It's reasonable to believe that every American alive on that day can still tell you where he or she was when Pearl Harbor was attacked. That was a shocker that still causes disbelief. The "day of infamy," as President Roosevelt called it, was etched into everyone's memory. We knew where we were and what we were doing when we heard the news. For most of us the reaction was that it could not happen, but then in the America of the late 1930s neither could we face the reality of such things as the bombing of Warsaw. We listened stupefied as we heard it described over the radio at the beginning of the war in Europe in 1939.

It was, after all, an alien war. Europe was infinitely

remote for most of us, a place our ancestors left to find a better life. With two weeks of vacation a year the norm for most people, a trip to Europe was unthinkable. The rich went there, and the American doughboys of World War I had been there, and most of them ended up back on the farm, despite having seen the "high life" of Gay Paree.

Most people said it was not *our* war. It was *their* war. Over there, in the Europe our forebears had fled to avoid precisely such turmoil and squabbles. Hadn't George Washington warned us not to get embroiled in foreign conflicts? And wasn't our founding father a veritable fount of wisdom?

In the Midwest, the doings of the Japanese seemed even more remote than events in Europe. We knew there was war in Asia. Manchuria and China had been invaded. Speakers on the "college circuit" of the day told us of the rape of Nanking, and we duly saw the famous photo of the abandoned baby crying on the tracks of the Shanghai railway station. As for Asia, we knew of it through the works of Pearl Buck, oil for the lamps of China, and stuff of that sort.

Given the shoddy goods the Japanese shipped to us in the pre-war years, it was hard to believe they could produce arms to match those made in the USA! They were capable of making cheap tin objects, paper fans and paper lanterns. That was the extent of what we knew, or cared to know, about our future enemy. The Japs were remote, inept, and not worth worrying about. It wasn't that we did not believe what we heard about the atrocities committed in Asia. The men coming from China had impeccable credentials: they were Protestant missionaries. What they described to us, however, were atrocities of Asians against

10

Asians. We were smug enough to think that *we* were immune from such things.

In Midwestern Ohio, we knew even less about the Spanish Civil War being waged in the same period. That violent prelude to the main bout between democracy and fascism gave Hitler and Mussolini the proving ground they needed for the Big Event to start a scant three months after the Spanish Republic was shunted into limbo by the victorious General Franco. On our East Coast, things were different. The Lincoln Brigade was very successful recruiting on campuses in New York, but then we Buckeyes always knew how radical people were in those strange places. If we couldn't support a Lincoln Brigade because of Godless Communism's presence lurking behind it, the average citizen knew too little about the Spanish Republic to mourn its death.

Nevertheless, some events were beginning to attract our attention on the Atlantic side of our continent. Early in 1940, Hitler's invasion of Denmark and of Norway was successful. The Allies failed to stop the Wehrmacht. That was shocking enough, but from the shocking to the unbelievable was not far off. The Blitzkrieg that began in May that year quickly brought what we all had assumed was the world's strongest army to its knees. First Belgium and Holland were invaded, and then France. The French armed forces were decimated by the Nazis. Within weeks of the German invasion, the swastika was flying over Paris, the dream city in one Hollywood film after another in our formative years.

Of course, it's easy to say now that we should have taken our heads out of the sand. Our time was coming, and those of us in our late teens at that time were murkily aware that danger was lurking in our country's future.

Roosevelt mesmerized us with his Fireside Chats about such things as Lend-Lease, but for most of us it was far more comfortable to listen to the isolationists, or better still to go to hear the big bands at the local movie palaces, and to jitterbug to Tommy Dorsey or Glenn Miller. If we worried at all, it was for our future in an America just emerging from the years of the Depression. Salaries were still low and jobs hard to find. Would we be able to afford college? Could we find work? That was a reality everybody accepted. We knew how hard it was to turn an honest buck. We also knew that the American doughboy had "gone in" in 1917 to save democracy and to prevent all future wars. It had stopped nothing. Europe was at it again, worse than ever.

And so on that Sunday, December 7th, we refused to believe. Pearl Harbor decimated by the Japanese? Not possible. Another starwars broadcast à la Orson Welles just to scare us, people said. Our military leaders and officers were too smart, too well prepared for shenanigans of the kind the radio spewed out that afternoon. It was only when the reports were repeated and the newspaper extras appeared with headlines of PEARL HARBOR ATTACKED that we knew, with stunned certainty, that we were at war. We read incredulously of one defeat following another. The fall of Corregidor and the atrocities in its wake were like a nightmare, one that didn't seem to end.

We can see in retrospect that our military brass could and should have expected something of the sort. Intelligence reports indicated that the Japanese were preparing a major military move. The reports went unheeded. We were Fortress America surrounded by two enormous oceans that no one would dare to attack. Until that Sunday in December. It was an unusually warm day in central Ohio, so warm that windows were open, and the radio reports could be heard out on the sidewalks.

The initial reaction was a great surge of patriotism, but along with it, a sense of apprehension. We did not doubt our eventual victory, but as the extent of the Pearl Harbor losses slowly became known our concerns and our disbelief grew. How could Americans be defeated and maltreated by a nation of grinning little people always bowing to one another? Weren't we the biggest and the best, a beacon to the world, the undefeated?

Obviously, we had been dangerously over-confident. We were ill-prepared, and that lack of preparation in the 1920s and 1930s cost us dearly. Our deficiencies, nevertheless, as the world was soon to know, were to be surmounted by an incredible vigor, hard work, and a pervading spirit of youthful cockiness. The inventiveness of the American mind that had studded the nineteenth century with scientific miracles went to work to build the armed forces that would transform weaknesses and shortages into a war productivity of staggering proportions.

Meanwhile, men and women were going into training all over the country. The machines needed men, and the men had to be trained for combat, for a myriad of responsibilities, and for the handling of the machines. The mightiest military apparatus the world had ever known was being built, and the mightiest invasion ever undertaken, it became more and more clear, would have to take place before the backbone of Nazi Germany could be broken once and for all. If the Japs and Nazis had started it, we were sure that we would end it on our terms. December 7th was a major defeat for us. Two and a half years later, we had our major triumph, D-Day.

If most Americans could remember Pearl Harbor day with clarity, far fewer could say where they were when the news of the Normandy landings came over the wires. That morning of June 6th, however, I and a large contingent of my comrades were moved bag and baggage into shipment barracks. Where we were going nobody knew, as usual in those days. We were at Camp Ritchie, in the mountains of Maryland, the training center for Ground Forces Intelligence. Hagerstown, quite a distance away, was the nearest urban center. Having had Air Force basic training a year earlier, I had the "good luck" to have to go through infantry basic training before my Intelligence courses could begin. That training was capped by a forty-eight hour exercise in snowy mountain-climbing, compass reading in the dark, and murky tents smelling of burned K-rations and sweating men. It ended with a lengthy crawl under barbed wire in a trench full of ice-covered water with live machine-gun bullets overhead. Cigarettes in quantity and the use of "son-of-a-bitch" as a mantra brought me through unscathed. Some seventy percent of my fellow trainees ended up in the camp's hospital.

While the physical part of our training could seem rough, the educational part of it was highly exacting but very stimulating. I had been sent to Ritchie after six months at Hamilton College in Clinton, New York, and had had an experience I dearly loved. Hamilton's Army Special Training Program was a top-rate one in which we had intensive work in French language, geography and customs in preparation for going to France, and where

14

there was also a group preparing to go into Germany. Despite the long and exacting hours of class and study and the military trappings we had to maintain, we were college students in khaki, in a beautiful campus setting. Ritchie was army barracks and often grim routine. We were not college students in khaki there, but soldiers with a clear purpose. We were getting ready to go into Europe. We learned to identify German uniforms and units, to read maps with accuracy, to use a compass, and to duck bullets. And to side-stroke for half an hour with an M1 rifle held above the water. We were taught techniques of interrogation for information. If Hamilton was theory, Ritchie was practice.

I hated leaving friends and teachers at Hamilton, but leaving Ritchie was like the opening of a new door. The only concern many of us had had before June 6th, either expressed or repressed, was the possibility of going into France in the first wave of landings. At the same time, the idea of being a part of one of history's greatest dramas, the invasion of Hitler's Fortress Europe, was an attractive one.

By June, we were certain we'd be heading for Europe very shortly. We were right. Late Tuesday afternoon the 6th, the loudspeaker in the shipment barrack came on. It announced that the invasion of Europe had begun on the coast of the Cotentin Peninsula of Normandy. We all cheered. The uncertainties were over. We were convinced that this would lead to the end of the war in Europe and in our total victory. That evening we boarded a train for Boston, where, after a short stay at Camp Miles Standish, we boarded the Cunard liner, the SS *Aquitania*, for a zigzag crossing of the Atlantic to the port of Greenock on the Firth of Clyde in western Scotland.

The Saturday before we left, I had a pass. A married friend from Ohio was stationed in Boston, and his wife and baby were with him. We had dinner at the elegant Copley-Plaza Hotel, and I broke the regulations to call home. It was the last time I would hear family voices for a long, long time, perhaps forever.

A few days later we were on the Atlantic heading for Britain. The weather was ideal, and the crossing was without incident. We saw not another ship all the way to Scotland. And, above all, no U-boats!

Clearly, the roadway to Berlin began in France. It was France that was the key and corridor to Germany. Normandy, directly south of England across the Channel, was finally designated, in Eisenhower's words, to be the "springboard" for the assault. The plan was given the code-name OVERLORD. By the time the brutal battle against the German U-boats had been won, arms, men, and matériel poured into England from across the sea, from Fortress America. We, like the English soldiers in France singing before the blitzkrieg of 1940, were determined and ready to hang out our washing on the Siegfried Line.

D-Day remains a fascinating story, no matter how often it is repeated. The preparations for the landings constitute a story in themselves. Every war buff knows about the Allied Intelligence ruses to keep the Germans guessing. Hitler became convinced, fortunately, that the landings would take place in the Pas de Calais area, which the Canadians had raided earlier with considerable losses. Miraculously, Allied G2's deception worked. The German High Command considered the Cotentin landings a feint, convinced that the real invasion would begin to the north. The error cost them dearly.

As all the history books on the war tell us, the Allied landings were initially scheduled for June 5th. According to the meteorologists, the night of the 4th–5th would be ideal. The tide rising at dawn would be advantageous in the demolition of underwater or beach obstacles, and high tide would allow the landing craft to come in with their cargoes of men, vehicles, and matériel, while moonlight would provide visibility for naval bombardments. But the best laid plans are subject to the unpredictability of nature. Severe storms made crossing the Channel and a rendezvous with ships from farther north an impossibility. Everyone was ready, but Eisenhower had to make the terrible decision to postpone the departure. He himself has spoken and written about his agony in those fatal hours of decision-making, when hundreds of thousands of men jammed into the close quarters necessary for the loadings into ships and planes had to wait under conditions of great tension.

What was happening in France itself is less known to English-speaking readers. Across the Channel, France was undergoing unrelenting Allied bombings. As rail lines to the target areas were vital to the movement of supplies and men to Hitler's Atlantic Wall, railway tracks and bridges were prime goals. It was decided, wisely, that the bombing of railroad repair shops and marshalling areas would be most effective. Rail transportation throughout central France and lines coming in from Germany itself could be crippled. The plan was effective, and was aided by French partisan forces, notably the FFI, Forces Françaises de l'Intérieur of the Résistance who mined both rails and bridges with impressive daring and success.

Eighty targets were chosen in France and Belgium, the

raids beginning in early March of 1944 with an RAF bombing of a town twenty miles to the west of Paris. There were 190 direct hits on the tracks of the marshalling yards, which remained out of operation for two months' time.[1] The Eighth US Air Force's raids were equally successful, and by the middle of May the wreckage was great enough to close traffic on major lines for ten to twelve days. By then fifteen marshalling yards were wrecked and forty repair centers for locomotives were badly damaged. The hundred trains a day from Germany required for the maintenance of the Wehrmacht in France had fallen to sixty in April and down to thirty-two in May.

A total of 430 locomotives had been wrecked by the bombings and another 1500 were immobilized by the end of May, reducing traffic to 13 percent of what it had been in January, thus seriously impeding the German efforts to move troops, workers, and supplies into the crucial coastal areas. The number of railway viaducts destroyed was 1,900, of highway bridges, 8,793. Throughout all of this the Luftwaffe remained surprisingly inactive. The anticipated raids or V-weapon attacks on southern England or London did not materialize. The attacks on the launching pads for the V-weapons by both air and French resistant fighters hampered their launching.

The results, plus Hitler's miscalculation of the landing site, were, we know, decisive in a victorious invasion of the Cotentin Peninsula, but they were not without their negative side, particularly for the French civilian population and the rebuilding of the vast regions devastated by the bombings and destruction, in Normandy first of all, but actually throughout France. Trains did not run for a considerable length of time. In moving with Third Army across France, we saw no trains moving until some time into November, after battle lines had been stabilized in the Lorraine area of the east.

As a train buff, I was acutely aware of the wrecked locomotives and freight and passenger cars on tracks or in marshalling yards. One afternoon, we sighted a luxury train of the Wagons Lits Européens abandoned down the tracks as we were driving in the country. It was worth checking out. The train had been heavily strafed, and there it stood empty in open countryside. There might well be some documents of interest left on board, we reasoned, but compartment after compartment turned up nothing. However rapidly the passengers had had to run for cover, probably in an adjacent woods, they had been fast enough to take everything with them. No cache of secret documents or stolen loot, just an empty train with most of its windows shot out.

We were warned to anticipate French resentment over the destruction of their towns and villages, but the surprising fact was that the French people, even in areas laid waste by bombs or ground fighting, greeted us with open arms. Bomb if you must, they said, but bring us our liberty again, even if the price must be death and destruction.

Saturation bombing, utilized primarily by the British as opposed to the precision bombing practiced by us Americans, was particularly destructive. The effect on French thinking resulted in a marked preference for us Americans that still finds vocal expression in some quarters in France today. There were no Yankee Go Home signs in those days. They came much later as the Communists gained ground all over France in the post-war period. There were none in the 1990s either. It was Welcome Veterans all the way.

Note

1. Statistics are taken from Chester Wilmot's *The Struggle for Europe*. New York: Harper and Brothers, 1952. This book remains one of the best and most informative of publications on the war in Europe. It is an invaluable source of information.

III

PATTON'S MEMOIRS, *War As I Knew It*, entitles the section on the campaigns in France in the summer and fall of 1944 "Touring France with an Army." It is a catchy title that describes much of what we experienced in the halcyon days of August when vast areas of French territory were liberated with relative speed, ease, and few losses, but things quickly changed when we got to eastern France in Lorraine and the Saar area.

Those sunlit days of a waning summer made war seem distant and even absurd, almost like the illusion we stubbornly held to that somehow we had already won the war. Mentally we had relegated the grime and sweat of battle to Normandy. That August we were in the chateau country, the land "flowing with milk and honey" and a considerable amount of wine. We were young, cocky, and victorious, even smug.

We also were deluded, but it took some weeks before we had to face that fact. We were not alone. The American public in their haven between the seas may have felt some tensions over marauding submarines off our coasts, but the publications of the period portray a robust, smiling, healthy people bursting with confidence. In his study of psychological and emotional expectations in the USA and

21

Britain, Paul Fussell in masterly style captures that psychological moment for those of us in uniform as well as the non-military public. The jeep had already become emblematic of the burgeoning confidence we felt, just as for many of us, the jeep still is the symbol of that war:

> Watching a newsreel or flipping through an illustrated magazine at the beginning of the American war, you were likely to encounter a memorable image: the newly invented jeep, an elegant, slim-barrelled 37-mm gun in tow, leaping over a hillock. Going very fast and as cute as a Bambi, it flies into the air, and behind, the little gun bounces high off the ground on its springy tires. This graceful duo conveyed the firm impression of purposeful, resourceful intelligence going somewhere significant, and going there with speed, agility, and delicacy – almost wit ... At first everyone hoped, and many believed, that the war would be fast-moving, mechanized, remote-controlled, and perhaps rather easy.[1]

Equally implicit in that kind of thinking was the use of air power. Certainly no one can deny the enormous importance of aviation in the conduct of the war. The Luftwaffe had darkened the skies in 1940 to the terror of the military and civilians alike. It herded urban populations onto the roads during the battle for France in ways that greatly complicated French military movements, sending thousands of civilians onto the choked highways in the hope of avoiding bombs on cities. It could strafe and it could bomb, but slowly top brass learned that it did not win wars alone.

That was another illusion we all shared. As Paul Fussell points out in his *Precision Bombing Will Win the War*:

The fact was that bombing proved so grossly inaccurate that the planes had to fly well within antiaircraft range to hit anywhere near the target, and even then they very often missed it entirely. As the war went on, "precision bombing" became a comical oxymoron relished by bomber crews with a sense of black humor. It became obvious to everyone except the home folks reading *Life* and *The Saturday Evening Post* that although you could destroy lots of things with bombs, they weren't necessarily the things you had in mind.[2]

Nevertheless, in the thinking of many a GI on the ground, the idea of aerial bombardment as a means of quick and relatively painless (to us) victory was very much on our minds as we watched squads of bombers flying overhead. We cheered and waved like a bunch of kids. We happily hailed the news of the destruction of enemy cities and their inhabitants. We usually forgot that most of the bombers flying over our heads were directed towards targets in France, Belgium or Holland, and that our allies rather than our foes were a part of the target.

Certainly the raids on French railyards, bridges, and repair shops had done a great deal in the cutting down on the delivery of German troops and matériel to the Channel areas, and no one can doubt that aviation was very much a part of the planning and thinking in preparation for the landings on the Cotentin Peninsula. In his book, *Victory in Normandy*, British General David Belchem writes:

23

There is no doubt that the most important single factor in the success of the invasion was the mastery in the air established by the Allied air forces before D-Day, and subsequently maintained throughout the operation. This dominant air supremacy had an adverse effect on every aspect of the Germans' defence philosophy, planning, conduct of operations and logistical capability ... Allied air power ... had obstructed Luftwaffe air reconnaissance to the extent that the assembly and Channel crossing of the massive armada of ships and craft had not only been unmolested but took place unnoticed until its arrival in daylight off the French coast. It had been an important element in the pre-D-Day Deception Plan, and had provided the vitally effective radar deception plan during the night of D-1. Its interdiction programme had immobilized the railways in the essential areas, and destroyed the bridges on the lower Seine and the Loire. It was only in the bombing of beach defences during the pre-assault stage that results were largely disappointing, due to the incidence of cloud and bad visibility, though where conditions were favourable, as at UTAH, the air attacks proved highly successful.[3]

The first Americans on French soil, moreover, were the parachutists of the 82nd and 101st Airborne Divisions. They had begun their landings at 0130 and 0230 hours, the latter with the assignment of taking the western end of a causeway behind Utah beach's formidable shore batteries and blockhouses, then of moving on to capture the small city of Carentan to the south-east, while the former was to secure the town of Sainte-Mère-Eglise, about five miles inland, and bridgeheads across the Merderet River.

Sainte-Mère-Eglise's liberation has been dramatically related in prose and film, and was duly celebrated in the ceremonies of June 1994.[4] The story bears repeating. The 82nd Airborne succeeded admirably in its mission of taking the town, but it was not without cost. Bad weather caused navigational problems for pilots who were in some cases getting their baptism of fire. As a consequence, drops were signaled far from target areas, gliders went awry, and men landed far from where they should have. In the Merderet region, men drowned in some three feet of water, dragged down by their parachutes and equipment. The First Regiment of the 82nd Division did, however, come down within three miles of Sainte-Mère-Eglise. By four o'clock the morning of June 6th, that community, then of some 1300 inhabitants, had the distinction of being the first town of France to be liberated from German occupation.

That is the positive part of the story. There was a cruelly negative side as well. American paratroopers who landed in trees were shot where they dangled on their parachute ropes. As a reminder of those killings, a parachute still hangs from the steeple of the church in memory of John Steele who fell onto the steeple, his own parachute hopelessly tangled. He played dead until two Germans cut him loose and took him prisoner. He escaped several days later. It was clearly a night of chaos as well as victory.

For all of us, the crossing of the Atlantic was a sort of introduction to the war. Books on the war frequently picture the *Queen Mary* as a troop ship. It may well have been the best known, but far from the only pre-war luxury liner converted for transport. The *Aquitania* on which I crossed in June 1944 sailed out of Boston harbor onto a sunny Atlantic all alone. No escort. Down deep in the hold in our tiers of canvas bunks, we were told that in case of a torpedoing, our section of the ship would be sealed off. For most of us, it was our first confrontation with a numbing truth: in wars, all of us are expendable. We realized how vulnerable we were. No exit except death, and that, really quite willy-nilly. If the ship was hit, we went down with it. A sobering revelation of one of life's basic truisms that until then had never dawned on me, or most of my comrades-at-arms. Despite death's presence as we plowed through the waves that early summer, we remained convinced that the war would be miraculously and quickly won.

The invasion that began on the night of June 5–6 was centered on five beaches on Normandy's Cherbourg-to-Bayeux sector. The northernmost, Utah, faced east into the Channel. Some two miles inland from it lies the town of Sainte-Marie-du-Mont, and several kilometers to the north-west of it, Sainte-Mère-Eglise. Utah, along with Omaha Beach to its east, was the target of US First Army under the command of General Omar N. Bradley. Beyond Omaha were the beaches attacked by the British and Canadian forces, Gold, Juno, and Sword. The paratroops, however, were on French soil some hours before the actual landings on the beaches took place. There were severe problems and losses in many sectors, but military historians have since pointed out that the chaotic descent in some areas proved to be an advantage. The Germans were totally confused by the spottings of parachutists here, there, and everywhere. Something of that confusion is clear from a rather humorous account of what took place in a small chateau, Le Bel Enault, near Sainte-Marie-du-Mont. It is now a charming bed-and-breakfast run by a French couple whose older son, just entering his teens, is already a WW II buff. He has even made an impressive war museum all of his own in the family farm's typically Norman stone barn.

On the night of June 5th, the chateau was occupied by its owner, an elderly lady, and her maidservant-companion. One of the lady's forebears had had a penchant for exotic plants, and finding that a quirk of terrain would permit the cultivation of tropical trees, had planted several palm trees around the manor, despite the often rigorous weather of the area.

THE STORY OF LE BEL ENAULT, JUNE 5 AND 6, 1944
or
EIGHTEEN PARACHUTES AROUND MY CHATEAU

On the 5th of June, 1944, German soldiers came by Le Bel Enault to tell Madame Blanchet, who at that time was the tenant living in the property then called the "chateau of the palm trees," that there would be manoeuvres that night with live ammunition and that cows left outside would not be safe.

At about 11 p.m. there was the sound of airplanes flying low over the rooftop. Small weapons fire as well as automatic gunfire could be heard. Then all was quiet until daybreak.

Next morning, Madame Blanchet did not want to go outside because there was a dead paratrooper lying in front of the main gate. When she looked out over

27

the swampy fields, she saw at least a hundred parachutes on the ground. That was when she realized
that that day had to be D-Day. She counted eighteen
paratroopers who had landed around the chateau.
One had broken the wooden bridge when he landed
on it.

The parachutist lying beside the gate showed no
sign of life. Another one had gone through a hole
in the roof of the house, and a parachute was left
hanging on the trees near the water. On the highest part of the chateau, another paratrooper had
succeeded by the aid of his straps in reaching the
ground without breaking his neck. The one who
landed back of the chateau in the garden of exotic
plants must certainly have thought as he looked at
the palm trees that this surely did not look like
Normandy!

Two German soldiers lay dead across the road,
supposedly killed by Colonel Johnson of the US
101st Airborne division that landed near Le Bel
Enault. No cooking fires could be built because
even the smallest smoke would have brought automatic weapon fire or even hand grenades through
the windows. Madame Blanchet was so frightened
she didn't know where to hide any more. The front
door had been broken down, Germans and US paratroopers went in and out of the chateau, jumping
through windows and shooting at one another throughout the halls and rooms.

Under fire, Madame Blanchet finally left the chateau
by crawling outside with a mattress for her protection. She was followed by her maid, crucifix in hand,

both of them praying, "Dear God, protect us." They finally ended up hiding in a toolshed at the back of the garden.[5]

The palm trees still surround the house today, and never fail to surprise the newcoming visitor. The mementoes of that night also still turn up now and then with most any digging around the house to remind us and the present owners of that fearful June 5th when the Germans ordered the cows to be called home!

By midnight of Tuesday, June 6th, the Allies held five sections of Norman beach along an area some fifty miles in length. Within the short space of twenty-four hours, miracles were accomplished. Over 156,000 American, British, Canadian and French soldiers were already on French soil, almost 133,000 brought by a fleet comprising more than 4000 ships, accompanied by over 1200 warships of various kinds, in all forty-seven convoys operated by 96,000 naval personnel. An extraordinary feat by anyone's criteria. Even repeated as cold statistics, the figures stagger the imagination.

By the same token, much that had been part of the initial planning had not been accomplished. Many objectives continued to be in German hands. The link-ups between beachheads were not to be made until June 12th. The plans counted on the capture of the strategic city of Caen on the first day. The Germans defended the town to the dust and only after thirty-four days of bloody battle did it fall into Allied hands. It was finally taken by General Montgomery's forces on July 9th. In the interim, men and matériel were poured into the rubble of Caen instead of being deployed to fight elsewhere. The plans called for the liberation of the important port of Cherbourg at the tip of the peninsula on a timetable of D-Day plus eight, and then of D-Day plus fifteen, but did not fall into American hands until June 27th. By then, the Germans had made the facilities unusable. The repairs caused further delay. The first convoy arrived on July 13th and the first four Liberty ships on July 26th.

By that time, the Cotentin had already been cut in half. Barneville on the west coast was liberated on June 18th, making the fall of Cherbourg inevitable and putting the northern half of the peninsula irreversibly under Allied control. By American geographical measurements, however, that area was still very small, maneuvering was difficult, and the enemy always close by.

By July 6th, one month after the invasion itself had begun, the Allied forces seemed stalled, but it was on that day, precisely, that the Battle of Normandy entered a mew phase. No one could have known it that day, but Operation Overlord would soon be back on track and moving toward its goal, the invasion not just of Normandy but of Europe. What had changed was a presence, that of General George S. Patton Jr., one of military history's most competent tacticians and certainly one of its most colorful, not to mention controversial, to this very day.

Patton was flown from an airstrip near his English Breamore House in Hampshire by C-47 to France.[6] One hour later his plane landed behind Omaha Beach, bringing with it the General, his English bull terrier Willie – named for William the Conqueror – his faithful Sergeant George Meeks with bedrolls and personal luggage, and a jeep. The General had reading matter with him as well: a volume of Freeman's study of William the Conqueror's preparations

30

for his famous storming of England in 1066. What particularly interested Patton was discussions of the roads utilized by William in both Normandy and Brittany. Despite all the intervening centuries, the terrain and road system was essentially the same. Patton would make good use of the information.

General Bradley welcomed him to his headquarters near Isigny. Third Army was to become operational at noon on August 1st. Patton was impatient, even suspicious that there would be some kind of delay. In the meantime, he and his presence in Normandy was top-secret. Even those of us in fields near by and in intelligence itself did not know the famous figure under whom we would soon be serving. An elaborate hoax had been mounted to lure the Germans into believing that Patton was assembling a major invasion force to cross the channel at the Pas de Calais area. A plan code-named Fortitude was concocted. The Germans were tricked into believing that Patton would head a force some 12 divisions. A "Potemkin village" of equipment, vehicles and troops was set up. It was all sham, a clever conglomeration of stage props, but the Germans were taken in. The German Fifteenth Army was held in place to defend the area from the highly respected, and feared, General Patton!

In the meantime, nobody was to know the general's real whereabouts or what plans had been decided upon for his future. Even Patton was kept in the dark about the latter.

The Germans had to be kept guessing. And fooled for a crucial length of time they were. Nobody was to know Patton's whereabouts or what plans had been made for his future. The Germans respected him and knew how aggressive he could be. They feared him. Was he across the

Channel from Dieppe, ready to start the real invasion of the Continent? The illusion was maintained.

Patton set up his provisional Third Army Headquarters in an apple orchard to the north of the hamlet of Néhou. It is hard to find Néhou on a map, even a fairly detailed Michelin one of Normandie Cotentin. If you weren't looking specifically for it, or had no sense of its modest role in history, you could easily drive right through it. Not even many French war students know about it. It is a hamlet rather than a village or town, with a church and a cemetery at its center, plus a few houses, one a manor house only recently restored through the offices of Patton's granddaughters Georgina and Helen. Just a crossroads, one might say, and yet it was a short distance north-east of Néhou in an apple orchard, that Patton and his army headquarters were set up in tents.

For many years a sign at a crossroad above Néhou identified the area as that of Patton's sojourn. No one seemed to know exactly in which field the general slept, ate, pondered and fumed as he waited to get into the thick of things. It seemed there had been a large farmhouse adjacent to the headquarters area, but no abutting town or hamlet where people might become curious about the famous personage camping out there. The hamlet and the field are situated almost directly west of Sainte-Mère-Eglise half way across the Cotentin, and fifteen miles almost due south of Cherbourg. Until the summer of 1994, the old roadside sign written in French and in English had proudly proclaimed that Néhou was the place where Patton first dwelled on French soil, but, as we know, that is not quite accurate. It was outside the town, in a tent, bedroll and all.

Robert S. Allen, colonel in command of Third's combat intelligence, gives his version of what life was like at that time in the Cotentin:

On June 9, SHAEF communicated two items: (1) that Third Army would be responsible for receiving Hq Ninth Army when it arrived in the UK around June 29; (2) that the Forward Echelon would be lifted to the Continent on D+29. As many Third Army units had not arrived, preparing and equipping them by that date presented a tremendous problem.

One thing topside was always generous about – laying hot potatoes in others' laps.

But Lucky was all set to roll on June 29, when the green light was received to move to Breamore Hall. And it also was ready four days later when the order came to head for the Cotentin ... July 4 and all that night the Staff moved slowly with hundreds of other motor convoys to the Channel. Early the next day it embarked for Southampton in LSTs [Landing Ship Tanks] and the following day went over the beaches.

That night the beaches were heavily attacked by German bombers. Two big ammunition dumps went up in exploding flames.

But Lucky was quietly resting in foxholes and trucks hidden in the deep massive hedgerows of Normandy apple orchards near Néhou, 15 miles south of besieged Cherbourg and six miles from VIII Corps' line of contact.[7]

Curiously enough, except in Allen's book, the stay at

Néhou is given almost no mention in the Patton books. Perhaps a canvas tent in a Norman orchard carried no glamour for so famous a figure, but since so many of us lived that same experience in Normandy in the first weeks after the invasion, we might call it a shared experience.

It was in this obscure little spot, however, that Operation Cobra was nurtured and what was eventually the *percée*, the "piercing" or breakthrough of Avranches, one of the most felicitous and exciting episodes of the whole war. In the first days of that July, things were not going all that well for the Allies. The terrain of the Cotentin proved very difficult with its hedgerows enclosing small fields, many with dense and aged growths of trees and bushes, in effect tiny breastworks that had to be assaulted one by one and that readily camouflaged snipers and German movements and equipment. As Allen points out, "the invasion was weeks behind the planned time schedule and operations had slowed practically to a standstill."[8]

Logistics also were a problem. The violent storms of June 19 to the 22nd had pretty much destroyed the artificial harbor at Utah Beach and severely damaged "Mulberry" in the British zone at Arromanches. What the Allies held was, in fact, little more than an extended beachhead, but what was also apparent was that the Germans still felt the major assault could come in the Pas de Calais area to the north and so had held the Fifteenth German Army unit intact above the Seine River. By the same token, forces were also being moved out of Brittany to reinforce units in the Normandy area. There was a great deal to be done, and little reason for Patton, as almost everyone writing about him at this time repeats, to be obsessive about getting into the war before it was over! He was soon to be in the thick of it, as was Third Army. July was a crucial month.

What was accomplished in that month as Patton languished in his tent? Caen, or what little was left of it, finally was in British hands on July 9th. Its capture had been a priority in the initial planning and was to have been under Allied control, along with Bayeux and the road to the strategic Saint Lô, by the second day of the invasion, D-Day plus One. The fall of Caen, however, resolved none of the basic problems. The Germans reorganized at the accesses to it and on the road to Falaise, directly to the south-east of Caen. The springboard to liberate all of France and head for the heart of Germany remained out of grasp. One assault after another in the attempt to break through to Falaise ended up with serious losses of men and matériel, while General Bradley, on the western flank, after taking the town of La Haye-du-Puits, also with considerable losses, realigned his forces on a line running across the peninsula from Lessay on the west through Périer on to Saint Lô, the ancient capital city of the *département* of La Manche and a vital communications center situated on a high rocky spur ringed by ramparts and turrets. It had been under almost constant bombardment since June 6th and subsequently earned the name of Capital of the Ruins. Nothing but the shattered towers of the Church of Notre Dame was left intact by the time it finally came into American hands on July 19th.

South of Lessay stood Coutances, another ancient cathedral city that was of strategic importance. It was a prime objective in Operation COBRA, set to begin on July 25th, but postponed until the next day because of bad weather.

The artillery bombardment and aerial bombings were staggering in their intensity. By noon of the 27th, the German line was disintegrating, and by the 28th, the VIIth and VIIIth Corps of the American First Army had taken Coutances.

In the meanwhile, Patton, almost 59 years old and bursting at the seams, so to speak, chafed at the bit. He was ready to move. Robert S. Allen says that he saw clearly that Brittany was ripe for the taking once a breakthrough had been made, and he wanted the opportunity to be the one to lead Third Army into what did soon become one of its glowing victories. Néhou had been a trial of patience and forbearing. According to Ladislas Farago:

Probably this was the toughest period of procrastination in Patton's life because he now had everything and yet nothing. The very location of his so-called Third Army Headquarters, in the idyllic apple orchard at Néhou, near the little Douve River, was symbolic of his paradoxical situation. High up in the Cotentin, it had been captured weeks before, on June 16th, by the 60th Infantry Regiment of Major General Manton S. Eddy's 9th Division. They were men of his own Third Army, attached to General Collins' VII Corps for the drive on Cherbourg. The war had left Néhou behind. Now only stray German mines and the junk-heap of the bygone battle's steel litter, neatly bulldozed off the roads, reminded him that he was in the combat zone after all.

At Néhou Patton had all the trimmings and paraphernalia of a major headquarters organization, not only his own, but also those of three of the four corps he would command when he became operational. Though the place hustled and bustled with the energy that always flowed from him, it was in reality a paper organization.[9]

While Néhou may have been a kind of wartime backwash, all around it in those crucial weeks of July battles were taking place, as we have said. It was not until the 27th of the month that Lessay on the west coast of the Peninsula and Périer to the east of it were liberated. The following day, Coutances was taken by 4th Armored Division. The move south was under way. VII Corps, with the Second and Third armored divisions, headed towards the resort town and port of Granville and beyond it the strategic city of Avranches, soon to be the axis on which the real liberation of France was to turn.

Patton himself says little about Néhou, but does follow his interest in ancient fortifications by noting the structure of the chateau of Briquebeque which had supposedly belonged to one of Julius Caesar's officers during the conquest of Gaule two thousand years before. He recounts the oft-told anecdote of the crossing of the bridge at Carentan, reportedly very dangerous because of German shelling, only to find four GIs sitting on it fishing. He also discusses the launching sites for the V-bombs, the situation of Cherbourg, the deaths of much beloved General Teddy Roosevelt, and of Colonel Harry Flint and General Lesley McNair, whose funeral had to be kept secret for security reasons. But Patton was busy thinking and planning in that little apple orchard. He had come to some important conclusions before he moved

37

south on the morning of July 31st to a point just north of Granville:

> I also read *The Norman Conquest* by Freeman, paying particular attention to the roads William the Conqueror used in his operations in Normandy and Brittany. The roads used in those days had to be on ground which was always practicable. Therefore, using these roads, even in modern times, permits easy by-passing when the enemy resorts, as he always does, to demolition.[10]

Patton was just about to inflict on the Germans the blitzkrieg techniques that had given them such striking victories over the Allies in the early phases of the war. He was on the threshold of glory and fame. He was also to be in the very thick of the fighting, as units of Third had already been as a part of COBRA in Bradley's First Army. The war on his doorstep he was so afraid he might miss, however, was to be in large part his from here on in. The "prima donna" was to have full stage. Patton's reiterated "L'audace, L'audace, toujours L'audace," was soon to be put into action.

Notes

1. Paul Fussell. *Wartime, Understanding and Behavior in the Second World War*. New York and Oxford: Oxford University Press, 1989. p. 3.
2. Fussell, *Precision Bombing Will Win the War*, pp. 14–15.
3. Major-General David Belchem, Head of Field-Marshal Montgomery's Operations and Planning Staff, 1943–45. *Victory in Normandy*. London: Chatto & Windus, 1981. p. 114.

4. In Cornelius Ryan's book *The Longest Day* and subsequently in the film of the same name.

5. From *The Paratroops at Sainte-Mère-Eglise*, Chapter 18. My new translation. This is left in each guest room at Le Bel Enault, the property of Monsieur et Madame Gérard Grandin.

6. Colonel Brenton G. Wallace in his *Patton and His Third Army* says that Headquarters received orders on July 3rd to move the following day south to the embarkment ports, 23.

7. Allen, Robert S. *Lucky Forward, The History of Patton's Third U.S. Army*. New York: The Vanguard Press, 1947, 74.

8. Allen, 76.

9. Farago, 443.

10. Patton, 89.

IV

GO BACK TO France today, and in almost every city or town you will find Rue Patton, Avenue Patton, Boulevard Patton, Parc Patton, Place Patton, or Hotel Patton, to the point that the General's name has become a kind of household word. Ask any French man or woman of any age who General Patton was and you get a smile and a quick answer: "Le général américain qui nous a libérés": The American general who liberated us.

Try that same question out on Americans. Veterans and older people certainly know the answer, but try it out on young people today. Asked if they know who Patton was, you'll probably hear an "Oh yes, I saw the film on TV!" Then try the sixth of June, 1994. Answer: "The film *The Longest Day*."

General Patton was indeed beautifully captured on screen by George C. Scott, and *The Longest Day* did the same for the invasion of Normandy. More recently, most people on this side of the Atlantic did see the parachute jumps of June 5th, 1994, on TV, and Presidents Clinton and Mitterrand laying wreaths at Utah Beach, but beyond that, there is little real evidence of interest in "all that old stuff." As a matter of fact, as with so much else in American life of our present time, the many war films on the television screen have transcended the reality. History as fiction can live on, but without that all-important transformation, events are quickly swallowed up in the maw of oblivion.

Yet the world those very young people live in would be a far different place if that invasion had not succeeded. One thing is certain: the liberation of Western Europe and the defeat of Nazi Germany would have taken vastly different shape had it not been for the presence of George S. Patton at the head of the US Third Army.

There is convincing evidence that had Patton been given more leeway and sufficient fuel for his tanks and vehicles, the war might have been shortened considerably and the demise of Hitler and his thugs brought about weeks or even months before the actual surrender, but more of that later on.

Few who know anything about him would deny that Patton was a genuine hero of World War II. Certainly no one in France where Third Army is proudly hailed as *l'Armée Patton*, Patton's Army. In his day, however, he was a highly controversial figure, much admired, much feared, and much disliked, and in the end, almost deified, to this day a legend and a cult figure among his men.

Look at the photos of him. The arrogance and the sartorial splendor leap out at us. Early on, he earned a reputation for being highhanded. At West Point, severity with his fellow cadets brought him little admiration from his peers, and all of us in his command knew his demanding discipline, down to ties, shines, and shoestrings. His own proclivity for special uniforms, ivory-handled pistols on both hips, and the like, established his image as a "dandy." Truman, newly become president, wrote in his diary in June 1945 that General MacArthur was "Mr. Prima Donna, Brass Hat, Five-Star," then lumped Patton together with him, with the clear implication that he saw Patton as a prima donna too.[1] A photo taken during the Potsdam Conference of July 1945 showing Truman with Eisenhower and Patton, the "prima donna," elicited the following description of the latter:

> the tall, theatrical Patton resplendent in buckled riding boots, jodhpurs, and a lacquered four-star helmet. Patton seemed to glow from head to foot. There were stars on his shoulders, stars on his sleeves, more stars than Truman had ever seen on one human being. He counted twenty-eight.[2]

This was not unusual for Patton. Others who have written about him, including his own officers who staunchly defend him and praise him, dwell on the General's need to cut a fine figure, in peacetime as in war.

All of Patton's biographers comment on the consequences of his actions and the rather bizarre image of him that was held by the American public, and even by his military peers, particularly after the "slapping incident" in Sicily:

> However, his superiors must not be blamed exclusively or even too strongly for not having given Patton the place in World War II his genius deserved and which he, if given the job, would have probably justified. When he arrived in England in January, 1944, to take part in "Overlord," he already had a number of strikes against him. In the circles where the ultimate

decisions were made he was regarded as a monumental bore and trouble maker who, it was reluctantly admitted, was indispensable.

Even so, it was not genuine disapproval of and mortification at his boisterous and thoughtless extra-curricular deeds that were instrumental in turning his superiors against him. Even Patton's slapping of two soldiers in hospitals in Sicily was initially regarded as an inevitable offshoot of his bizarre methods of command, and was attributed to his highly emotional dedication to his job. It came to be considered intolerable only when it produced a scandal.[3]

What Patton's superiors concluded was that this was a man who had to be kept in line, reined in from his own excesses. This was done by various means, by direct orders sometimes, but also by assigning troops, supplies or matériel to other armies or army groups.[4] In World War II, Eisenhower generally supported Patton, but the "feud" between the latter and Field Marshal Montgomery did sometimes end up with the Englishman's winning out, to Patton's disgust and rage.

Eisenhower recognized clearly that Patton was temperamental, rash, and touchy. He was very concerned with the question of naming Patton commander of Third Army, as Omar Bradley would be over him. Bradley, usually considered the brain behind many an army operation, had been a subordinate of Patton's in North Africa. In "Overlord," as the upcoming invasion was called, Bradley was to be Patton's superior. Eisenhower's concern was unfounded, fortunately. Both men accepted their new relationship without problems. With Eisenhower as coordinator, Bradley as the thinker and planner, and Patton as the brilliant and often mercurial executer and tactician, the so-called trio that was to forge the armed forces that would bring about the reconquest of Western Europe and the crushing of the Axis was in place.

The weeks leading up to Patton's promotion and naming to the leadership of Third Army were painful and uncertain ones for the General himself. On the very day of his triumphant reception in Palermo as victor over the Germans in Sicily, the infamous incidents of Patton's slapping and abusive treatment of two hospitalized soldiers came to a head. Eisenhower had tried to keep the matter quiet and "in the family," but the famed New York columnist of acid tongue, Drew Pearson, broke the news and a political firebomb was launched. From the halls of Congress to the homes of the humble and the parents of the ordinary GI came cries of outrage and demands for Patton to be ousted as a commanding general. Significantly, Patton makes no mention of the incidents, his public disgrace or his private trauma; perhaps they were too painful to recall or write about.

As it was, he was relieved of command in Sicily and then sent off on a kind of tour that included the western Mediterranean areas under Allied control, Egypt, and the Holy Land. Had it not been for friends in high places who recognized his astonishing military potential, the future commander of Third Army and the hero of its exploits might have remained on the shelf, a spectator rather than its leader to victory after victory.

In *War As I Knew It*, Patton does describe a good bit of his tour, and he does so with relish and intelligence. His comments on the hygiene of some of these areas would hardly please the inhabitants of today, but much of his comment and observation makes for interesting, if colorful, reading. He saw history with a soldier's eye, relating his 1943 sightseeing to ancient times and ancient battles. What comes through is an Anglo-American of his time who is by no means insensitive to history, and one who was chafing at the bit while he was doing this traveling.

By the same token, the soldier-general was fully conscious that he and the staff accompanying him constituted nothing more than a kind of decoy to keep the Germans guessing as to what he was up to and where he might fit into the patterns of the upcoming invasion of northern France. As Patton had been an avid reader of military history since childhood, he enjoyed snooping around ancient battlefields and fortifications that he had read about but not seen:

> The places he [Patton] was visiting were soaked in history, and his strange assignment gave him the first and only opportunity in his life to see them. Yet he undertook the trips in a restive mood because he, unlike the Germans, knew only too well that he was not to be given command of any of those fronts.
>
> By the time he reached Italy early in January, 1944, he was deeply depressed. He was condemned to watching his colleagues Mark Clark and Alfred Gruenther up to their necks in war where he had to play the part of the visiting fireman.[5]

In the meantime, at home in the USA, the controversy over Patton was raging. Senator Bailey of North Carolina demanded that the General be court-martialed, his pending promotion had to be held up, and serious questions were raised about the "culprit's" fitness to lead American soldiers in battle. His professional abilities were not, however, ever seriously in doubt, even among his enemies.

If Americans on the home front wavered in their reaction to their temperamental and unpredictable general, however, the Germans had no doubts as to the threat that he posed to them. Before the end of January, 1944, German intelligence services had concluded that Patton would be a part of the leadership of the invasion, but he was also still associated with Seventh Army in Sicily. Suddenly, he disappeared from German reports. It was not until late March when it was announced that Patton had "relinquished command" of Seventh Army that German intelligence assumed he was in England.

He was actually installed in his new Third Army headquarters in an area between Manchester and Liverpool in an ancient and impressive timbered manor house called Peover Hall. He lived there in the manner of a country squire with his sergeant, and his pet Willie. He also had most of his favorite staff there working with him. He had requested the transfer of men close to him in Seventh Army, and was successful in getting the officers he wanted: Gay, Harkins, Maddox, Cummings, Muller, and Oscar W. Koch, who was to prove invaluable in his direction of Intelligence operations.[6]

Very few of us, if any at all, knew the history of Third Army. It didn't occur to us that our unit could have existed before us, and be it said that we *did* transform what was hardly a glamorous organization into a famous entity. Third had been formed in France in 1918 just after the Armistice that ended World War I. From France it was moved to Germany as a part of the armies of occupation until 1919. At that time, it was deactivated and its personnel reassigned. Third Army ceased to exist for over a decade, but that original army did leave its mark. Being originally an army of occupation gave the subsequent form of the shoulder patch its design. The encircling O of the patch stands for Occupation, and the A for Army on the now famous red-white-and-blue circle.

It was in 1932, when the United States was divided into four army sections, that Third Army was reconstituted. Headquarters alternated between Atlanta, Georgia, and Houston, Texas. Coincidentally, both Generals Eisenhower and Patton had been assigned to Third when it was under the command of Lt. Gen. Walter Kreuger, who became known for having formed one of the best training armies of the time. Another officer who had also been part of that training was Courtney H. Hodges, commander of the Third into 1944 when its status was changed from that of Training to Combat, on December 31, 1943, when it was also alerted to the fact that it would be sent to Britain for participation in the invasion of Europe. Hodge's relief of command was kept secret, as was Patton's naming to the position. In *Lucky Forward*, Colonel Allen recounts how there was a near slip of the highly secret information: In a bundle of mail he [Headquarters Commandant in the USA] found a letter addressed, "Lt. Gen. George S. Patton, Jr., CG Third Army, APO 403, Postmaster, New York, N.Y." On the envelope was the return address of Patton's wife![7]

In 1944, a small contingent of officers and enlisted men of the recently activated combat army were duly sent via the *Queen Mary* to Europe. On arrival in Scotland they were met by the newly named commanding general, "Old Blood and Guts" himself, and then taken by Major General Lee's private train "lent" to Patton for the occasion to Peover Hall to begin preparations for the mighty number of troops soon to begin following across the Atlantic. Organization and planning were quickly under way, in all areas required for the coming operations on the Continent. All staff were given very strict orders to maintain secrecy as to their commander.

Even at this point, however, Third Army might well have ended up with someone else in charge. Things had not all gone well for Patton thanks to his impetuous tongue and irascibility. As a result, his hold on Third looked tenuous for some time.

Patton had been summoned to Algiers on January 22nd, 1944, for reassignment in the United Kingdom. It was the day of the landings of Allied invasion forces in Anzio and Nettuno in Italy, soon to be the site of great bloodletting and misery. In almost four months of entrapment on the beach, there were some 59,000 casualties, which, with hindsight, it is now generally conceded, could have been avoided had the original commander moved quickly off the beach before German units could be reinforced and moved into strategically advantageous positions. It was no doubt strongly in mind as planning went forward for D-Day and, above all, it was a grim reminder of what could all too easily happen to invasion forces.

It had been almost exactly a year before, January 23, 1943, at the conference in Casablanca, ironically enough hosted by a Patton whose victory in the Operation Torch invasion of Morocco had been followed by a less than savory acceptance of Vichy collaborators,[8] that Roosevelt

48

and Churchill came to several very important decisions: the Atlantic was battlefield Number One, more aid was to be sent to the Soviet Union, and preparations should proceed for an invasion of France. The latter was not to take place in 1943, however, as Stalin was insisting. Sicily was to be next instead.

Although top brass assumed that the slapping incidents in Sicily were relegated to the past, another matter arose that threatened Patton with removal from his new command. It too involved the Sicilian campaign some six months previously. During landing exercises at which Generals Marshall, Eisenhower, Bradley and Lucas were present, Patton had lost control of his temper. He cursed and belittled the men involved to such an extent that his fellow officers listened in embarrassed silence.[9] The episode might have been glossed over, without affecting Patton's future, but another incident came to light that added to the general's diminishing reputation off the battlefield. Two of Patton's men, a Captain Compton and a Sergeant West, were court-martialed. Both were accused of killing Germans who had surrendered. Their justification was that Patton himself had so ordered in cases of sniping and certain types of enemy resistance. They pointed out the general's own remarks in a public address to his troops before the battle.

By now, the question whether Patton could survive all of this controversy and still be named to the high command he so desperately craved was a moot one. Controversy swirled around him as he was ordered to go to England in January 1944. He had been reprimanded. Even worse, he suffered the humiliation of having to make a public apology to his troops for his transgressions. Consequently, it was reasonable to assume that the troubled general would carefully avoid further conflict off the fields of battle. Patton apparently intended to do just that, but ill luck pursued him. Another incident occurred in England, despite the general's good intentions. It took place in the small town of Knutsford in Cheshire.

Patton had been assigned an apartment in London. His first visit to it has a distinctly humorous side to it. The dwelling he was taken to was the former apartment of a lady of dubious reputation and obvious profession. The boudoir decorations, complete with mirrored ceiling above the oversized bed, must have caused many a chuckle behind the aggressively masculine general's back. On the other hand, he had nothing to complain about in the manor house assigned to him in the country. It was called Peover Hall in Over Peover just outside Knutsford and is next to the small church of Saint Lawrence where Patton regularly worshipped during his almost six-month stay. Given Patton's love of history, plus his pride in the English ancestor his grandson Robert has traced in his excellent study of the Patton family, the church, parts of which date back to the early fifteenth century, was sure to please him as much as the manor whose "lord" he temporarily became.

Peover Hall was the seat of the Mainwaring family from the early twelfth century, and the main building, dating from Elizabethan times, now restored by present owner Randle Brooks, was a suitable place for Patton to entertain the many friends he soon made in Knutsford. The great hall was made for entertaining, and entertain Patton did, as he and his wife had done lavishly in the USA during the period between the two great wars. He also was seen in town to do some shopping, with Sergeant Meeks, his black orderly at the wheel, and his dog Willie, in their jeep, as some Knutsford residents still recall.

It is not surprising then, given Patton's sociability, that a local women's group asked him to come to speak to them at a ceremony to welcome the increasing number of GIs stationed in the area. The lady heading the ceremonies, a Mrs. Constantine Smith, assured Patton that there would be no reporters and no photographs if he consented to speak. With her assurances in mind, Patton agreed to make some informal remarks thanking the ladies for their thoughtfulness in caring for his men. He also spoke of the Anglo-Americans' destiny to rule the world after the war, making no mention of any participation by the Soviet Union, then our ally. At the time, it was a serious political gaffe. The storm broke. Congress was up in arms. Patton had done it again! It was not until early May when Secretary of War Stimson intervened that Eisenhower sent Patton first a telegram and then a letter confirming the command of what was to become known evermore as PATTON'S Third Army.

The date and time Third Army officially became operational was noon on Tuesday, August 1st, but Patton had already been operational through his position as deputy commander of VIII Corps under General Troy H. Middleton. The strategic hub of Avranches, with three major roads converging on it from the Cotentin to the north, and flaring out to its south into Brittany on the west and central France and the Loire valley on the east, was the indispensable key to a breakout. There were two natural obstacles to Avranches, however. Just to the north of the city runs the Sée River, and just to the south, below a bend with a clear and unencumbered view of the soaring medieval abbey of Mont Saint Michel, is what could have proved a serious obstacle, the Sélune River with its two upstream dams. The latter was, and is, spanned by a bridge dating back to Roman times, a fact that had not escaped Patton's attention.

Two bridges over the Sée were captured on Sunday, July 30th by units of 4th Armored which then entered the town. A German counterattack began that night, and a withdrawal was ordered, and so began a seesaw battle that was to last for some days and result in the pulverizing of whole areas of the city. On Monday, Patton held his last staff conference in Néhou, exhorting his men to advance constantly, pushing the men in order to avoid casualties, and leaving the guarding of army flanks to the enemy. At 11:30 that morning also, "Lucky" became "Lucky Forward" as the headquarters and its general moved south by the village of St. Sauveur-Lendelin near Bréhal to the north of the Granville-Sartilly-Avranches highway, N 173. 6th Armored had taken Bréhal a day earlier and it was now Command Post of VIII Corps.

General Oscar W. Koch in his *G-2: Intelligence for Patton* tells us that Third Army's drive through Avranches was

an intricate maneuver from the outset. Down the west coast of the Cotentin (Cherbourg) Peninsula, troops of two Third Army corps streamed simultaneously through a narrow corridor to get "around the corner" – west into Brittany, south toward the Loire, and east toward Le Mans. Two main north-south coastal highways were the only routes available, and these converged at the Avranches bridge to form a single roadway for a distance of about five miles. It would become known, appropriately, as the "Avranches Gap."[10]

It was the bridge mentioned earlier, Pontaubault, or as sometimes also written, Pont Aubaud, crossing the Sélune River close enough to the sea to have clear markings of the point to which the tides rise. American and British sources do make mention of the bridge, but it is French sources that have pointed out the great importance of that bridge's existence – intact – in the incredible unleashing of Third Army into Brittany and the Loire valley area.

Today, a new and more modern highway bypasses Pontaubault, but there is a clear view of it from the bridge further on, also bypassing the charming little village that huddles just beyond the original bridge. Apparently the Germans overlooked the strategic importance of that crossing point until it was too late to blow up either the bridge or the dams upriver. Either one could have been disastrous. Severe flooding would have held up the breakthrough by at least a week, and possibly more. In that length of time, often fatal in a war of mobility, battles have been lost and victories turned into defeat.

The bridge did hold, however, and division after division crossed it and headed southwest or southeast. The real invasion could now take place. It had been spearheaded with the "percée" or "piercing" of August 1st. In seventy-two hours, French sources tell us, the bridge became the sieve for the massive descent into France: 100,000 men and 15,000 vehicles, including the Second French Armored Division of General Philippe Leclerc. The impossible had been made possible. Patton's audacity had succeeded, but still the route of that success depended on one single bridge and one single road.[11] That bridge was vulnerable, and it could also have been used by the Germans had they retaken it. The Germans did not take long to recognize the seriousness of what was taking place and counterattacked in force, hoping to retake and hold Avranches and to staunch the flow to the south.

Notes

1. Quoted from HST Diary of June 17, 1945, *Off the Record*, in David McCullough. *Truman*. New York: Simon and Schuster, 1993. 399–400.
2. McCullough, 428–9.
3. Ladislas Farago. *Patton, Ordeal and Triumph*. New York: Ivan Obolensky, 1963. 503.
4. See Farago, particularly 504. The question of diversion of supplies and matériel appears repeatedly in writings re the problems of the battles in eastern France in the fall of 1944 in all of the books consulted for the historical description of events I discuss in this section. My principal sources are: Farago, Colonel Robert S. Allen's *Lucky Forward, The History of Patton's Third Army*. New York: The Vanguard Press, 1947, and Chester Wilmot's *The Struggle for Europe*. New York: Harper and Brothers Publishers, 1952, and Patton's own *War As I Knew It*. New York: Houghton Mifflin, 1947, and reprinted in various editions by Bantam Books as a "Bantam War Book."
5. Farago: 363.
6. Brenton G. Wallace, in his *Patton and His Third Army*, Harrisburg, Pa. and Washington D.C.: Military Service Publishing Company, 1946, lists the full staff of Third U.S. Army Headquarters as of the summer of 1944 and spring of 1945 on pp. 21–22, as does Charles M. Province in his *Patton's Third Army*, New York: Hippocrene Books, 1992, pp. 15–16.

7. In Allen, p. 15.

8. A lengthy and detailed description of Patton's role in Morocco can be found in Farago's chapter entitled "Proconsul in Morocco."

9. Farago, p. 410.

10. Brigadier General Oscar W. Koch. *G-2: Intelligence for Patton.* Co-authored with Robert G. Hays. Philadelphia: Whitmore Publishing Company, 1971, 63.

11. *Numéro Historique: Juin 1944, La Bataille de Normandie*, in *Paris Match*, No. 792. 13 Juin, 1964, 86.

V

THAT BRIDGE OF Pontaubault was indeed vulnerable. What the history books do not make clear about Avranches or the bridge is the jeopardy in which the now famous breakthrough remained for some days. The Germans did counterattack, despite the severe losses they had sustained in the American offensive of July 25th. On the morning of that day, all German units called through the same message: aerial attacks in successive waves, with destruction of bridges and artillery positions throughout the central Cotentin area. Then all phone lines went dead. The reason was that more than 2000 bombers had turned some four miles by two into a veritable inferno. In a space so small, the result was a ratio of one plane bombarding for every few yards. The result was that within twenty minutes, over half of a German force of some 5000 men of the armored division were dead, severely wounded or buried alive in the debris of what had been tanks and artillery pieces. COBRA had indeed struck with success.[1] Then, in their turn, even the Americans were stopped by the resulting chaos. When they moved forward, they found themselves faced with a lunar landscape. Only bulldozers could force their way through the jumble of bodies of men and machines, the bomb craters and shell holes, the uprooted trees, and the fallen walls. Shortly after, German General Beyerlein, on hearing orders that not a single man was authorized to leave his position, countered angrily to the messenger that all of his men would certainly remain where they were: all of them had died at their posts.

This destruction had facilitated the initial American capture of Avranches and the beginning of the phenomenal movement of troops and vehicles across the bridge into Brittany and the Le Mans-Loire region. The single bridge and a single roadway from Avranches south led to the prong of two routes, one into Brittany to the west and the other into the "belly" of France to the southeast. Patton had acted with the audacity that made him famous, but such a narrow corridor for his troops to pass also involved great risk.

Marshal von Kluge had had his forces decimated by COBRA, but he recognized immediately that the recapturing of Avranches and holding it had to be accomplished at any cost. Otherwise, the cornerstone of the German forces' "angle" would be in enemy hands. He even declared, with a certainty that events subsequently bore out, that the loss of Avranches meant the loss of the war in the west. Pontaubault had become the *nombril du monde*, "the world's navel."[2] To recapture it meant more bitter fighting, more bloodshed, and additional martyrdom for Avranches, which had already undergone severe destruction.

Going into Avranches today, it is hard to imagine the rubble to which it was reduced. There are reminders of the war and of the role the city played in it, but they are hardly much more in evidence than monuments found all across France. The most easily identified one is the impressive

Place Patton, the memorial on the large circular square where presumably Patton himself stood, urging the vehicles of Third Army on through the town to the south where officers and non-coms in their turn motioned and shouted to keep the trucks and jeeps and armored vehicles fast moving over the essential kilometers of the narrow gateway towards victory. The soil and the trees on that plot of ground are from the USA, and the land itself is American territory. Nearby is a modest but pleasant hotel called Hotel Patton. The only other clear reminiscence is the great empty area separating the site of the ancient cathedral, where a plaque commemorates Henry II's penitence for the murder of Thomas à Becket, and the very beautiful, and peaceful, Botanical Gardens with its splendid view of Mont Saint Michel. Anyone knowing how crowded together medieval cities and towns in Europe were is struck by that vast area, which, of course, was all built up until the bombardments and fighting of 1944. Other than that, the city has been remarkably well rebuilt around those buildings and monuments that were still standing after the battles had moved on.

French sources list Avranches as having a population in 1944 of 7578 inhabitants.[3] Of that number, 6390 were left homeless as 1850 buildings were destroyed or heavily damaged. The hamlet of Pontaubault is listed with 281 inhabitants, with nearly 80 percent of their homes destroyed.

The bombardments of Avranches had begun as early as June 7th.[4] The tracts dropped by the Allies urging the French inhabitants to seek shelter outside the town had fallen on the outskirts and so were ineffective. This resulted in severe losses in people and in buildings that night. That was just the beginning. The bombardments, usually from Flying Fortresses, continued almost daily, particularly near the railroad station, until July 31st. Most of the Germans, however, had withdrawn on June 7th, and almost 6000 French civilians left their homes for the countryside to avoid the bombings and strafings, which, in the hunt for the enemy, actually were taking place with little respect for city or town. Furthermore, people on farms or in farming villages stayed put to care for their livestock. It was not unusual to see French civilians wandering about where actual fighting was taking place! This meant, however, that the rubble of Avranches itself was practically abandoned by soldiers and civilians alike. We Americans did not know that.

July 30th, 1944, was a Sunday. The Catholic faithful in the immediate vicinity of Avranches had postponed First Communion ceremonies because of the bombardments, but decided that the time had come to go ahead that fateful day in the adjacent village of Val-St-Père. At Vespers, the ceremony hardly begun, the attack by Middleton's VIII Corps got under way. The church trembled and shook to the sound of the artillery and the planes that swooped near the steeple. The ceremony was cut short, and as the children and their families came outside, they were astonished to see the 4th Armored Division's American tanks with their white star. They had crossed the Sée River to the north of Avranches without combat. The bridge was untouched, and the Americans were as surprised by the lack of German resistance as the French by the felicitous arrival of their liberators.

The very next day, however, the field grey uniform was once more evident in the town. The Germans had returned. Four Sherman tanks were left burning by the Sée River.

Other American tanks to the south ran into a powerful column of the enemy coming up from Pontaubault, favored by a rain and mist that hampered American air action. The American commander, General Dager, wondered if he could hold out. The situation continued to be grave until around noon when the sky cleared a bit. A squadron of P-47s soon put the German forces to rout, and some 100 prisoners were taken. Avranches itself was a cataclysmic sight, its streets choked with dozens of vehicles of every kind overturned or incinerated. Horses ran about the ruins in panic. Nor were the Germans ready to give up this strategic point of land over which enough troops quickly passed for the 4th Armored to reach the city of Rennes to the south and the 6th, after bypassing Saint-Malo, to move into Dinan.

On the 2nd of August, the German counterattack began. The Battle of Mortain got under way. General von Kluge was determined to reoccupy the narrow corridor of Avranches and to cut off the American Third Army. Throughout the battle, German planes bombed and strafed the city and the area, and the recapture of the city remained a very real threat. On the 7th, the enemy was close enough that its artillery was clearly audible, and motorcyclists came quite close. Mortain itself exchanged hands seven times, and by the end of the battle on the 12th, Mortain, like so many of its Norman sister cities, had been, for all practical purposes, obliterated from the map. The liberation of France from the Nazi yoke was assured. The flow of men and materials into France would grow ever greater.

As I have said, the bridge at Pontaubault today is quiet and rarely used. The busy traffic goes on the new road, across the new bridge. The village is charming in the August sun, people eat lunch in a nearby garden, a flock of sheep lie taking an afternoon siesta in the shade of the railroad viaduct on the north bank of the Sélune. A pastoral scene that would have served a Watteau or a Fragonard as a perfect setting for their airy depictions of courtiers reveling in the peaceful countryside. A plaque on the bridge's end speaks as much about the various incarnations of the structure from Roman times to our own as about the astonishing accomplishment of that passage of some 100,000 men and 15,000 vehicles in the first seventy-two-hour period.

Closer inspection of the ground below the railway viaduct does yield evidence of war. Pieces of stone and metal are embedded in the earth, debris from the bombing which crippled the northern span of the structure, leaving wholly a third of it dangling to the ground, as photographic archives from August, 1944 show.

What I remembered from the day our jeep sped over the Sélune was not the bridge itself or the river, but the sight of that famed medieval miracle called Mont St Michel. The brief glimpse of it from the curve just below the city as we headed towards Pontaubault stayed with me until years later when I finally got to see it. That day in 1944, however, an incredible line of vehicles stretched in front of us as far as we could see, all heading towards the city of Le Mans. The fumes and dust were such that we put on our gasmasks and kept them on until we got to the chateau on the city's outskirts where we were to spend the night.

How we knew enough to get there, I have no idea, but we did. Things had been clearly planned. Our jeeps, the two assigned to my Team 443 with its two officers, Captain Roland H. Breton and First Lieutenant Rolf Armer, and four non-coms, Earl O. Coon, Audace "Joe" Previtti, Charles Jennings, and myself, pulled into a large grassy park-like area.

Before we left Avranches, a new officer, First Lieutenant and soon Captain, Roland H. Breton, had been assigned to us. He was from New Hampshire. He replaced Second Lieutenant Henry R. Hammond, who had been assigned to Military Intelligence Interpreter Team 116, dated June 6th, 1944, and therefore from the day of departure from Camp Ritchie, Maryland, for Camp Miles Standish outside Boston. Hammond had been particularly nice to me. I can recall chatting at some length with him in our quarters in the vast New Forest to the immediate southwest of Southampton while we awaited shipment across the Channel to France on a Liberty ship some time around mid July.

The previous June, the Atlantic crossing on the *Aquitania* had been as exciting for me as any pre-war cruise could have been for someone more sophisticated. Through Lieutenant Hammond, I had been put in charge of the ship's message center. What I did was sit at a table on the top deck and send "runners" to different parts of the ship with whatever official messages had to be conveyed. It was a cushy post, both because of its situation high above the dismal and boring hold where we sat and slept on tiers of bunks, and because I could see the light and the sea. I could also go to the front of the chow line, and recall my shock at taking food for breakfast only to find that I had a tray of kidney pie. I also heard stories of bombing on England, and particularly the savage raids on Liverpool, from the British crew, firsthand information from eye-witnesses that made the blood and suffering of war seem very real.

Being on the Atlantic had been an exciting experience for an Ohio landlubber like myself. The Channel crossing was no disappointment either. The weather was splendid. Neither a cloud nor a plane in the sky. The water calm, and so we sprawled about deck taking sunbaths until we approached the coast of France. There we saw a spectacle the like of which many a writer has described, but never fully captured, a panorama of ships as far as the eye could see, and as darkness fell, the "fireworks" of artillery and dogfights in the distance that lit up all the distant sky. We finally climbed down into the dingy hold with its high tiers of bunks. The next day would be our own D-Day.

As I remembered it, the weather that July morning began with sunlight, quickly clouded over and began to rain in gusts, then just as quickly turned to sun again. I thought perhaps my memory had tricked me, but twenty years later in 1964 when I returned to Utah Beach with Paul and Lucille Bougenaux, we had the same experience. As we stood on the high promontory overlooking the sea in the American Military Cemetery at St. Laurent-sur-Mer with its marble crosses and stars of David, the rain swept down swiftly followed by the sun that glittered on the sea and waves below.

Lieutenant Hammond knew how much I wanted to be the first to land on French soil, and so he told me to go on ahead of the team. I must have climbed down a rope ladder with all my equipment, but I can't recall it. We carried our duffel bag, arms, and ammunition with us whenever we moved, so that having a jeep with a bit of space for our belongings was a luxury.

At any rate, that morning in July, I climbed down onto a landing craft by myself among a shipload of vehicles, and we headed for a long floating ramp that stretched out from the beach.

As the landing craft neared the ramp, an officer yelled at me to get up on one of the trucks, and so I dutifully climbed, complete with all my equipment, onto the cab of what was probably a Chevrolet 4 × 4. It was almost my undoing. The front of the landing craft lowered and the truck started down onto the dock, but the driver turned to the left rather than straight onto the loading ramp, the front left wheel went over the edge, and I was tossed forward. Had the driver not reversed immediately, I might never have set foot on French soil. Instead I was thrown back onto my precarious perch, and landed, wet from rain but not the "drowned rat" I might have been.

I soon joined my comrades in the back of a truck that took us through a battered and empty Ste Mère Eglise and on, no doubt into the area near Néhou where our famous general was already secretly ensconced, to the apple orchard that was to be our home for some days. With our team of six was the detachment of fourteen men of Counter Intelligence Corps under the command of Major Edwin Bennett with whom we were to work throughout France until, after the Bulge, German MI teams took over for the final phases of Third's victory in the Third Reich itself.

Notes

1. Figures for this section are from the *Paris Match* special edition (Numéro Historique), 101.

2. *Paris Match*, 102.
3. From *Voie de la Liberté, Guide historique et Touristique*. Fontenay-aux-Roses (Seine): Imprimerie Bellenand, 1947, 108–9.
4. The sources for much of this information re the fighting in and over Avranches come from works by local historians: Alfred Marie. *Avranches, souvenirs de l'occupation et de la liberation*. Avranches: Editions de l'Avranchin, 1949, and Jean Séguin. *Bilan de guerre en 1944 dans la Manche*. Avranches: "Chez l'auteur réfugié" (n.d.). I was also shown albums of photos in Avranches of the state of the city at the time of the breakthrough. I am particularly thankful to Monsieur Leservoisier and his colleagues at the Mairie and Municipal Library for sharing material with me.

VI

THAT FIRST day in July 1944, or rather my first twenty-four hours in France, brought war's unpleasant realities home to me a second time as well as at the landing. Once in our new "home," our own little hedgerow field, we duly set up our pup tents. Each of us had one half. We had been particularly warned to look out for German snipers. The hedgerows were usually four to six feet high, and consequently offered abundant cover for the enemy. Dawn, we were told, was the most dangerous time of all, as the waning dark and waxing light made perception doubly difficult. We were to draw straws for our watches. It was my luck to pull the short straw: I got dawn!

It seems melodramatic, but that afternoon and sleepless night, I felt real apprehension, the fear that I wouldn't acquit myself well either protecting my comrades or facing the enemy. After all, I had never fired a gun of any kind except on the training fields. Could I shoot straight? And fast? I figured I'd soon find out. Darkness slowly and almost imperceptibly turned to light. The fearsome dawn came and went without a single incident. I'd done my guard duty without a hitch. I was alive and well in Normandy, France, and so were my comrades.

Life in the orchard field was not very exciting. We all

did a lot of smoking in those days, and we must have talked a lot. We also had those little Army paperbacks to read. But as one of the French speakers, I had a privileged situation. I talked with the local farming people and got fresh food for us that otherwise we would not have had. I also got to know a farm family that had a large old stone house nearby. I was invited to several succulent meals of food cooked "peasant style" in a huge iron pot hanging in a great open fireplace.

One day an official photographer who must have been with a headquarters group in an adjacent field asked me to go with him to see what could be photographed. He had heard that Granville was freed. I would act as interpreter. We left our field for the open road and hitched a ride in an Army truck as far as Granville, the old resort town on the coast north of Avranches. We walked to the port area, but were warned not to go out onto the dock area as it was still completely booby-trapped and mined by the Germans. Nearby was a small shop. The owner bade us welcome and exchanged a small bottle of Chanel #5 and two wooden painted brooches for some cigarettes. Something for the homefolks. My mother kept them all these years.

On the main street of the town, truck after truck full of GIs sped by. This must have been July 31st, the day of Granville's liberation. The city was not dormant for long, it seems. French war correspondent Jacques Kayser – a nephew of Alfred Dreyfus whose treason trial and subsequent vindication had torn French society apart in the early years of our century – notes in his notebook journals that he was in Granville on Tuesday, August 1st. He was amazed to find hotels open and already filled with British and American newspapermen. Back again on Saturday,

August 5th, he tells of dinner with Frank Capra and Ernest Hemingway.[1]

My photographer buddy and I were not as well informed. We did not know it yet, but the breakthrough had begun. But then one of the facts of our situation was that we were very ill-informed in our little hedgerows. We did not even know that Cherbourg had been liberated, an event that had taken place as early as June 27th. In our isolated field, we heard a rumor the city had been freed and that we would be trucked up there to have hot showers. That much was accurate. We duly had our showers in tents set up for that purpose. It was a welcome relief after the icy cold baths we had got used to taking in the small streams nearby.

As we nosed around Granville that day, we had no idea that Patton was close by or that we would soon be speeding into central France. An elderly woman stood crying on the street. She had had nothing to eat for two days. My shouting to the trucks to throw out a chocolate bar or two went unheeded. The noise of the speeding vehicles drowned me out. There was nothing to do. All my photographer friend and I had was cigarettes, and unfiltered at that. We wandered up the street to what had been a café before its façade had been blown off. The upright piano was still intact and on it stood the sheet music of a French popular song entitled *Ça sent si bon la France*. I played, we sang, and then walked to the road to hitch a ride in a farmer's pickup truck run on gasogène. Miraculously, we found our own fields, and went our separate ways. I never saw the photographer again, nor any of the photos.

At about this time, our MII and CIC teams moved south to another field, an orchard without hedgerows. It was north of the Sée River off the road between Sartilly and Avranches. As was customary, we dug two trenches, one a slit trench for nature's needs, and the other to jump into in case of strafing by the Luftwaffe. We did not anticipate the latter, and so rather lazily carried out our chore. We did not dig very deep.

Perhaps we were what Jacques Kayser called us: Boy Scouts. The American soldiers he had come in contact with, he writes, were very quick to jump into a ditch at the slightest gunfire. In our case, it was just the opposite. As I recall, it was the second day in our new orchard, late sunny afternoon, that we noticed strange lights in the sky. We quickly realized we were under fire. The lights were tracer bullets from German planes beginning the counterattack to recapture Avranches. That night, we found the trenches far too shallow, but finally crept into our pup tents to try to sleep on earth trembling from nearby bombardments. The next morning, we got out the shovels and went to work with a will and a way. Our immediate danger was over, however, but fighting went on all around.

Several days later, our team got a new commanding officer, Roland H. Breton. His role in the story of Pontaubault and of Avranches is a unique one. Breton told us that he had been hiding in a cellar during the bombardment of Avranches, but it was not until recently, at a reunion in Boston after forty-eight years, that he filled in details. Breton, then a First Lieutenant, drove with a major into Avranches, only to find that the Germans had returned and held most of the city. Breton got out of the jeep to reconnoiter, but when he returned to the square the major had driven off without him, deserting him in a town again swarming with the enemy. Breton passed three days in a cellar, including the night of the bombardments we had been made so aware of in our field. When he got back to his unit, he sought out the major and told him that he would shoot him if he saw him again. The major disappeared. Breton never saw him again. By someone's prudence, he had been transferred to another unit.

Breton's involvement in the events of those few days could have been of more than a cursory brush with history. He had been sent with a demolition squad to blow up the bridge at Pontaubault. The wiring was already in place. The structure had to be kept from the returning Germans. Before the fatal moment, however, word came through that the Germans had been pushed back. The bridge was saved intact for Third Army's advance. Old Blood and Guts could move his army south, and hurried to do so. One of military history's most spectacular campaigns was under way.

North of Avranches in mid-peninsula was the cathedral city of Coutances, liberated after fierce fighting on July 28th. The town had suffered severe damage from bombing as well as the fighting. I had a personal tour of the cathedral and what was left of the city. Lieutenant Hammond, the officer who preceded Breton as head of our team, had somehow gotten to know a priest from St. Pierre Lanyers, a hamlet near Sartilly. Half a century ago the hamlet was a center of considerable military activity. Its chateau had been requisitioned as a hospital by the Germans, and once in our hands it became an American hospital. The nearby fields were filled with GIs, both white and segregated black units, and there was even an orchard where movies were shown.

Movies were after my time in the area. And no films for the enemy. Local residents recall that during the fighting, the fields at the crossroads were so crammed with German corpses that it was impossible to walk across the ground.

The village priest, the Abbé Deshoyes, had a house guest, Father M. Lelièvre who was the *chanoine* or canon of Notre Dame of Coutances. Canon Lelièvre had not been back to his beloved church since the bombings and the battle. Would we drive him back to see what damage had been done? The three of us took off over the little country lanes and finally reached our objective, some twenty miles away.

We entered a silent and eerily deserted town. The destruction was frightening, and all three of us feared the worst. When we finally reached our objective, we found the houses around the square empty and in varying degrees of damage, but, miraculously, the cathedral had escaped unscathed. *Dieu soit loué!* One of the finest examples of Norman Gothic architecture was there in all its glory for us to admire and for the Canon, with great pride, to show his two GI visitors. It had survived its most fateful moment in seven hundred years of existence.

After this gratifying inspection of his fief, and no doubt the recital of a few prayers of thanks under his breath, the *chanoine* set out down the street to the empty shell of his house. He sought out a shovel and proceeded to dig in the garden back of the house. There, he soon located and unearthed three vintage bottles of red wine. These, he told us, would not go to the Germans. One for the three of us then and there, and the other two for dinner at the Abbe's parish house, topped off with Calvados, that powerful *trou norman*, to expedite our digestion.

The village priest's house still stands where it was, a few yards from the church, inhabited now by a farming family. The good curé, like his friend from Coutances, is still fondly remembered by some of the villagers who were a part of his flock in those far-away perilous times. They even unearthed an aging photograph of the good Father.

The cathedral was the first one I saw in France. I knew we could not mention any place names, but I was sufficiently impressed by what I'd seen to want to write home about it. I saw no harm in including some architectural details in my V-Letter, but the censor, I later learned, did not agree. The letter arrived home with line after line struck out. Barely comprehensible. Did the censor find my observations too accurate? What did the cathedral have to do with Patton? No doubt it was just that Third Army was such a top-notch secret that any hints had to be exorcized. We could not have told; even we did not yet know who our illustrious commander was to be.

Both priests have gone to their eternal reward by now, of course, but people still remember them with affection, and Christian Coupée and I were warmly received and shown a curious notebook kept by the Englishwoman companion of a French noble lady. The two women invited many a GI from all over the USA to come and eat at the manor house in the country near to St. Pierre. They left touching testimonials to the thoughtfulness of the ladies, but also to the kindness of the French people, who despite the destruction and damage to their homes and cities were all out in their welcome.

We would expect as much for the French themselves who came in with our armies. Jacques Kayser was one of them. There is much of interest in his account and much that foreshadowed what those of us in Intelligence would encounter as we moved on from Normandy. On the positive side was the exhilaration and the welcome of the French people themselves, lining the roads with flowers and bottles of wine in hand, cheering and calling out to us, the V for Victory on waving hands of adults and children alike. The dark side was also soon a part of our daily affairs. Not everyone was overjoyed to see us as victors.

The welcome mat remains out in Normandy. We found in the 1990s that the persistent myth of French hostility to Americans did not hold true at any point, from the museum by Utah Beach at St-Côme-du-Mont where veterans are shown every courtesy, to the other war monuments and museums, Avranches, Bayeux, Cherbourg, Omaha Beach, Pointe du Hoc. We found genuine pleasure in greeting veterans who come back. The Levaufre family in Périers is a case in point. Husband Henri Levaufre is the representative of the 80th Armored Division. His wife works with families throughout the area in arranging lodging for American veterans and their wives who return for reunions. Professions are matched to professions, so that despite language barriers, shared work experiences make communication possible. We were astonished at the Levaufres' World War Two memorabilia, and at their warm hospitality to three total strangers. Périers was also severely damaged in the fighting of late July, although you would not know it today.

Third Army officially became "active" on August 1st at noon. Our Intelligence teams became active a few days later. Our first assignment was in Vendôme in the *département* of Loir et Cher. It is a fairytale city to the north of

Blois on the Loir River and just south of the direct route from Le Mans to Orleans.

Note

1. Jacques Kayser. *Un journaliste sur le front de Normandie, Carnet de route juillet août 1944*. Paris: Arlea (n.d.) Kayser's on-the-spot observations are of considerable interest. The journalist himself, however, had difficulties in getting permission to go into Normandy, first of all, and then in getting accredited. It was not until July 14th that SHAEF accredited Kayser as Public Relations Officer, but then had to go to SHAEF in Normandy to get permission to carry out his mission, a prime example of the confusion caused by the reticence of the Allies to officially recognize De Gaulle.

VII

THE JOURNEY described in this book happened almost by accident. I had talked about going out to the landing beaches every time we went to Paris, and one former student of mine, then working in Paris, said he and his family would love to drive us out to spend a day or two in the Cotentin area. Before the trip could be realized, however, my potential chauffeur was transferred to Athens, Greece, a bit out of the way for a drive to Normandy.

Finally, in 1991, it was through close friends in Spain that the trip became a reality. We set out with Bob and Graciela Graber, who lived up the street from us in Segovia, Spain, heading for France. Graciela particularly wanted to visit the chateau country, which I had not been to for some time. I was also becoming more and more determined that sooner or later I would revisit *my* France of 1944, from Utah Beach in Normandy to Saarguemines on the German border and Luxembourg City. All four of us wanted to visit famed Mont Saint Michel.

We set out in August, heading for Bayonne across the border in France. We were there by early afternoon. We found a lovely city of rivers, old houses, beautifully stocked shops and stores where employees spoke in soft voices in marked contrast to the customary cacophony south of the border. Our modest hotel, a Michelin choice, was comfortable and a part of a tower in the ancient city walls. We had an excellent dinner with light French white wine. All very civilized in a charming setting. We found Bayonne far more appealing than neighboring Biarritz and even booked rooms for our return trip.

From Bayonne, we headed north through the Médoc wine area. We had made a wise decision to buy food in *charcuteries* every day that weather permitted and to have picnic lunches along the road. That particular day, we ate in a park on the banks of the Garonne in the wine center of Paullac. We loaded up with several bottles of Bordeaux red, visited a winery, took the ferry across the mouth of the river to Royan, and on to dinner and the night in La Rochelle on the coast. Another delightful town, pleasant people, great seafood, and a port area with its fourteenth-century towers straight out of a fairy tale.

The road north from La Rochelle towards Normandy was two-lane to Nantes, with many a traffic light in villages to tire and exasperate. We certainly could not make it as far as Utah Beach that afternoon, and would be lucky to get to Avranches in time to keep our hotel rooms for the night. We did so, however, with time to spare. Up the street past a couple of impressive antique shops was the Patton monument and square I hadn't known existed, with its high steel and stone spokes, like rays of light or points of a star, on which were carved the names of the cities and towns liberated by us in 1944. And beside it, a Fourth Armored Division Sherman tank, commemorating the day Patton stood at this very spot in the rubble urging vehicles southward in the famous breakthrough. Even the earth around the monument is American.

On one side of the square stands a modest but pleasant hotel. It is named for Patton. Its owner, as might be expected, is a great admirer of the General and of Third Army. He cordially invited us to have an aperitif in the lobby. He welcomed veterans and lamented the fact that more had not returned to Normandy, something that was to be remedied in 1994!

Back down the street, dinner at our more modern hotel proved to be far more traditional than the hotel itself. We had snails, a filet of pork cooked in Norman cider, cheeses, and raspberry charlotte. We men opted for an after-dinner Calvados to celebrate our arrival in the home of French cider and its more potent derivative.

The next day was the real beginning of the recapturing of time past. It started with reminiscing and filming at the monument to Patton. A stone's throw away, by the curbside, stands a *borne* or roadside boundary stone marking the beginning of the Route of the Liberation that begins just inside the tank wall at Utah Beach and extends to just beyond the American memorial on the outskirts of Bastogne in Belgium.

Then on to Mont Saint Michel for a tour of that extraordinary monument rising out of the sea, the traditional omelette lunch, and more video filming. Back on the Peninsula, we drove north to Granville where, on that July day so long ago, an army photographer and I hitchhiked down "to see what was going on." As most of the town was cordoned off for bicycle races, we had to enter from the north, whereas in 1944, my entry had been along the coast. Getting to the port area was difficult, and by the time we reached it, even stretching the imagination did not help.

We had a Perier by the port area, then headed north along the apple orchards where I had "lived" up the Sartilly road, Coutances and the landing beaches area.

During the drive up to Avranches, Bob Graber had asked me if there were "bed and breakfasts" in France. He and Graciela had lived in England for several years and had frequently used them in the British Isles with very happy results. I replied that I did not know, as we had usually stayed in Paris either in modest hotels or in the home of friends. Soon, however, we did see some signs, in English as well as in French. Before leaving Avranches, we got in touch with a bed-and-breakfast near Carentan, on the east side of the Peninsula. It was a felicitous find, in comfort, location, and hospitality.

We stayed at Le Bel Enault, a mansion or "chateau" that the Grandin family was in the process of restoring, and had already transformed into a very agreeable hostel, a *chambre d'hôte* or *gîte*, as the French call this. We were also just six kilometers from Utah Beach and even closer to the villages of Saint-Côme-du-Mont and Saint-Marie-du-Mont. The mansion, and particularly the gardens surrounding it, had a curious history. A nineteenth-century owner had had a particular interest in exotic plants. We had been startled as we drove up to see palm trees in the yard. We were not the only ones to be surprised, just as the American parachutists described in the account of the landings around the house the night before D-Day must have been. But more of that later.

Going to Utah Beach was a soul-searing experience. Tall grass now covered most of the tank wall. There was the main breach with the first of the Liberty Way markers. Next to it stood the small museum with an LST, tank and vehicles parked outside it. Then, a stroll to the north, was the second break in the wall, still identifiable, where the ramp on which I landed had extended out into the water and where I had come near death. Then on to that extraordinary monument to the Rangers at Point du Hoc, its bomb craters and ruined bunkers left as they were that fateful D-Day; Omaha Beach, with its monument; and then the great white sea of crosses and Stars of David at Colleville Cemetery. We stood in silent awe, tears streaming down our cheeks. I had indeed returned. I had not thought I could be so moved.

Our first night at the Grandins' house, we went to a farm nearby for dinner. The owner was a young woman who had a small but excellent restaurant in her family home that she operated only during the summer. That particular night as we were enjoying our dinner, we watched a large group of parents and children gather in the garden at the back of the house. It was all very orderly, the children exceptionally well-behaved. It was the owners' two brothers and their children. As we were finishing our dinner, our hostess asked if we would like to hear the children sing. We replied that we would and settled back to hear what we assumed would be a nice but impromptu performance. In came the children with their parents, very politely shaking our hands and introducing themselves individually, after which they went on to give us an astonishingly beautiful concert.

All of this was from those from those reputedly inhospitable French, who could not have treated us with more warmth and hospitality. As did Monsieur Grandin when we got back to our lodgings. He had waited up for us to offer us a tot of Calvados as a nightcap.

What, I wondered, would our reception be in the Loire valley area? Would we be greeted with indifference, even with the semi-hostility some Americans complained about after visiting France? Now that I had revisited Utah Beach, Point du Hoc, and Ste-Mère Eglise, I was curious about going back to Vendôme and Blois.

We had driven through Vendôme in 1974 on the way from Nantes to Paris. It was my only junket back in time until the 1990s, despite frequent trips to France in the intervening years. After a bit of driving around Vendôme, we had found the little Hotel Saint Martin where I had been billeted thirty years earlier. We went into the hotel for lunch. There was the picture-postcard bridge across the way, just as I remembered it, but the hospitality was hardly the overwhelming one I recalled when I arrived by jeep.

The owner in 1974 was a woman. We were seated in the dining room that had been decorated with the garlands and German songs of the Soldatenheim. I explained to our hostess that I had been in Vendôme the first days of the Liberation and had been billeted in the hotel. She seemed singularly unimpressed. She did, however, in a rather matter-of-fact manner, offer us an aperitif as a kind of welcome back. I had wanted to go upstairs to see the room I had stayed in and still remembered, see that kitchen where we crowded around a radio to listen excitedly to the news that Paris was free, but the attitude of "madame" did not invite either exploration or conversation. We ate our meal, paid our bill, drove about town a bit and hurried off to Paris where we were expected for dinner. Patton, his army, and the Liberation thirty years earlier surely was not on the mind of anyone we ran into in Vendôme that summer's day. Nineteen-forty-four seemed very remote, buried deep in the quicksands of time.

If we were to judge by that experience, we could expect now to be just four more tourists, but whatever happened, we had found the formula of bed-and-breakfast. Phone calls were made from one home to another, and we were passed on, first to a wonderful fifteenth-century house in Savonnière south of Tours, and then to the Cossons just outside Blois on the Loire.

Going to the Cossons was the chilling kind of coincidence that changes life's direction. I was quickly swept back to the war and the Liberation. Our reception was astonishing. The past began to come to life again with an inconceivable vividness.

VIII

THE DATE THAT Third Army became officially operational was August 1st, fifty-six days after D-Day.[1] My MII Team was number 443 and the CIC Detachment with which we worked from Normandy into Germany and Luxembourg was number 332. The date given for our first fully official duties was August 14, 1944. That was the day we arrived in the small city of Vendôme on the Loir River, a tributary of the larger and better-known Loire River (in French, respectively, *Le Loir* and *La Loire*). The same day, we stopped in another small city, St. Calais, situated on a direct route to Orleans, which lies directly south of Paris on the Loire River.

Orleans had been designated by Patton as a strategic objective, and several men of our CIC unit were sent in jeeps as advance guard in front of Fourth Armored tanks as they advanced into the city. There was some gratuitous bitching when the men came back to Vendôme, but no one was hurt, and as Fourth Armored men were known to bitch at us in Intelligence for "interrogating" them for information, one could say we were even. Fortunately, there had been no mines in the streets, but the city center was badly shot up, and shelling continued from the German positions on the south banks of the river.

An order "to secure Orleans as soon as possible" had been given in the city of Le Mans, the first major stop after the breakthrough at Avranches. G2 had reported that there were no Germans north of the Loire as far as St. Calais, about a third of the way between Le Mans and Orleans. 4th Armored Division was to lead the way. Particular attention was to be paid to Vendôme, just south of that main road, where contact with Engineering C Group was to be made, and Chateaudun, both towns a bit farther on to the east.

Our two Intelligence teams had gotten as far as the outskirts of Le Mans the night of August 13. I knew the name of the city from newsreels of the famed auto races that took place there every year before the war. That year of 1944, only we GIs were the racers. We had two audiences: the French and the fleeing Germans. One was exultant; the other, we were certain, had already lost the race. Our teams' destination the next day was to be Vendôme.

The general order about Orleans had been given orally by Patton on August 12. He confirmed it in writing on August 13 saying: 'XII Corps (4th Armd. Div, 35th Inf Div, and supporting troops) will concentrate southeast of Le Mans prepared to operate to north, northeast, or east, protect south flank of Army.'[2]

Our corps, composed of the 4th Armored Division and the 35th Infantry Division, was the southernmost or right-flank unit, and we remained so across France. To the south of us, on the other side of the Loire River which we would soon approach, was what has been estimated at from 60,000 to 120,000 German troops.[3]

By August 13th, what little was left of the city of

Avranches was finally in our hands, although the final phases of the Mortain counterattack by the Germans and the closing of the Falais Gap were not to be over until the 19th. The destruction and devastation for the Germans was serious; they lost about half a million men and vast quantities of equipment and matériel, thanks in large part to Hitler's stubborn intervention.

For us, at any rate, the way seemed open, except for problems of fuel shortages due to our rapid advance, a matter that would return to plague Third Army in Lorraine in the coming fall. Patton, nevertheless, was on the move, into Brittany to the west, towards pivotal Le Mans to the east, and then either on southeast towards the Loire or northeast toward the greatest prize of all, Paris.

The road from Avranches into the French heartland was two-lane. We took up both, our jeeps and vehicles stretching before us as far as the eye could see. It was hot and the dust was so terrible that we put on gas masks as a protection against it. When we finally got to Le Mans, or near it, after being part of one of history's biggest traffic jams and most brilliant military breakthroughs, we pulled into a large park area outside a small chateau. The grounds were already well filled with other vehicles, but we staked out space for our own, ate something and settled down for the night in our bedrolls in the tall grass.

I felt sick. That was something that happened to me on long hot trips when I was a kid, and here it was again, happening to an adult and a soldier! Fortunately, Captain Breton had a practical medical sense. He wisely suggested a shot from that great green jug of Calvados, a gift to us in Normandy that had taken up half the back seat of one jeep. It helped, within seconds, and so I went sound asleep on the silky grass. The next morning we were on our way, first to St. Calais, and then to Vendôme to "settle in" for several days.

Recent investigations have failed to determine just where that chateau of Le Mans was, but Dyer does indicate that two chateaux were used outside of the city proper:

> It was a still pretty green corps headquarters that fumbled its way into the bivouac areas southeast of Le Mans on the night of 13–14 Aug 44. Forward and Rear Echelons were set up under canvas in the grounds of two separate chateaux, along an important highway and a narrow gauge railway. The Fwd Ech CP was about seven kilometers outside the town. It "was right on the front line," as Maj "Ed" Johnson recalls it, "and they were even taking PWs out of the woods nearby. There were machine guns firing at the edge of the woods. The corps was really green.[4]

What could have been serious then, however, looks quaint and amusing with hindsight:

> The Rr Ech was going through much the same experience, according to Lt. Col. Clarence Bistline: "We heard a rumor that there were some Germans loose, and we sent some people out to hunt them. Bill Styles was with them. They didn't find the Germans, and lost Bill. When he was finally seen he was shooting rabbits. Later we did get six prisoners, and we were so green that we had about four men guarding them."[5]

The Germans had been billeted in the chateau itself before our arrival, and apparently had moved on in a hurry:

> The people in the Fwd Ech remember the huge chestnuts and other trees of the chateau grounds in which they camped, the signs of recent German occupancy, the piles of uniforms abandoned in one of the rooms of the chateau by German soldiers who had apparently sought to flee in civilian clothing. Those of the Rr Ech think of the old lady in the chateau who greeted them so cordially, and the hurrah's nest the Germans had left which she was trying to get cleaned up. And everybody remembers the yellow jackets or bees: "There were always 15 or 20 bees on every jam pot at mess. We used to try to decoy them by putting a jam pot about 15 yards away, but it never worked. The bees simply covered both pots," says Maj "Shep" Shepard.[6]

Despite fatigue and the confusion of getting things organized starting at 2 a.m. August 14, XII Corps headquarters was functioning by time for coffee and food. Our training period was over. This was the real thing:

> This shot was for the record, and the information was pitifully small compared to the "General Situation" and "Special Situation" of the training problems. The general feeling in staff sections was incredulity that you could know so little of the situation, have so few troops (if the troops got there), and still have an impending battle on your hands.[7]

86

That same incredulity at knowing so little about what was going on in general terms was to follow our Intelligence teams across France. We knew what was happening in our own sector, but frequently knew little about the overall picture until at least a day or two later, after events had taken place.

On that very day of the 14th, Patton's orders to secure the city of Orleans were to result in XII Corps' first battle with the Wehrmacht. The bridges across the Loire between Blois and Orleans were to be demolished to protect XII Corps' southern flank, and bridges on to the west between Tours and Orleans were to be prepared for demolition as well. The reports indicating that there were no Germans as far north as St. Calais were faulty. German units had not yet crossed the Loire to the south, but G2 did not have that information as yet.

From St. Calais to Vendôme is a short drive today, but took a bit more time due to the traffic problems that busy afternoon. Not knowing the roads, plus the time factor, made distances seem longer, and, of course, roads in those days were narrower and often not as well paved as today. We had stopped in St. Calais for some chow around noon on August 14th, and that afternoon got into Vendôme. In the main square of St. Calais, jammed with vehicles of all sorts, a young couple with a baby girl in arms and a little tow-headed boy, had came up to me. After establishing the fact that I could speak French, they asked if they could photograph me with their two children. I, of course, said yes. The couple's name was Chesneau. Their daughter was Nicole and their son, Guy. They dutifully mailed the photo home to my mother in Columbus, Ohio. The picture is dated on the back: St. Calais 14 août 1944.

When we got into Vendôme, crowds of people gathered around us in the square to welcome us, as they had in St. Calais. There was great excitement. We brought with us not only liberty but also a feeling of security. Fortunately, we did not learn until several days later that the Germans had returned to the area after our "triumphal entry" and more or less surrounded the town. We were unaware of it if true, and felt sufficiently self-assured to ignore such information as delusory boasting on the Germans' part. We were secure, and the French we were in contact with felt secure. Except for some *collabos* and domestic shortages, the war for Vendôme was to all purposes finished.

Vendôme is an ancient city, dating back to Neolithic times, long before Caesar conquered Gaul. The charm of its picturesque and venerable houses and buildings is enhanced by the River Loir's channels which make of the town a kind of miniature Venice, a "City of Water and Flowers," as tourist brochures proudly proclaim. It is situated more or less in the center of France, in that *douce France* of gentle rivers, broad fields and vineyards, and the chateaux of the wealthy and the nobility, past and present. One chateau near Vendôme is that of Count and Countess Michel de Rochambeau, he a direct descendant of the French marquis who fought with us in the Revolution and active member and former president of the Sons of the American Revolution in France. The statue of Rochambeau graces the main square just in front of a wood-beamed house of the fifteenth century in the center of town.

In addition to Rochambeau, Vendôme also lays claim to Honoré de Balzac, although he was not a true son of the city. At the age of eight, in 1807, the famed novelist was sent to Vendôme to study in the College of Oratorians.

The school's discipline was so severe that he retained a lasting hatred for his experience there, and given his indifference to his education, no one could have predicted that this youngster would later become one of the world's best-known writers. We can only speculate how he would feel about being touted as a "product" of the school he detested, but no one can deny that, for better or for worse, he spent several years studying there by the banks of the Loir. The chateau Balzac inhabited as a man in the village of Saché is not all that far on to the south-west. If he didn't like his schooling, he did continue to love the region throughout his life.

Another famous writer born in Vendôme's vicinity, Pierre Ronsard of the fifteenth century, is now considered one of the Renaissance's most important poets. Vendôme also proudly proclaims his presence in the city.

Naturally, this historical and literary material was not foremost on our minds on the afternoon of our arrival. As we have said, the formal date of the liberation of Vendôme is August 14, the day of our teams' arrival.[8] Photos taken that day attest the jubilation and welcome given to the first jeeps and tanks of our forces to arrive there. Throngs of people, young and old, gathered around us as we pulled into the main square, La Place Saint Martin, unintentionally, beside the socle on which Rochambeau's statue had stood. Hands reached out to shake ours, to touch us, and, of course, to accept American cigarettes, chocolate, and whatever else we had to give out. People who had never smoked before tried it in those first heady days of freedom. Interestingly enough, the ardor of that first day did not seem to diminish during our stay in Vendôme. Crowds gathered nightly before the hotel to sing the *Marseillaise* and to shake our hands. *Liberté, Fraternité, Egalité* could finally replace Vichy's *Travail, Famille, Patrie* (Work, Family, Country). The second occupation of Vendôme by the Germans – the first had been during the siege of Paris in the Franco-Prussian War of 1870 – was over.

A photo taken that day in 1944, like the one from St. Calais of me with the Chesneau children, shows me and my jeep surrounded by youngsters. The date was written on the back of the snapshot and sent home to Ohio. In the picture, right in back of us is the timbered fifteenth-century house before which Rochambeau's statue had stood. It was that building which made identification of the site easy even forty-eight years later.

In 1992, a poster with *AVIS DE RECHERCHE; OUI SE SOUVIENT DE CES VISAGES?* (SEARCH NOTICE; WHO REMEMBERS THESE FACES?) was put up in various parts of the city and run in the local newspaper by Christian Couppé of Blois. Two of the boys of the jeep photo, now in their fifties, came to the Liberation ceremonies of 1992, and the widow and daughter of another, dead for several years, also came forward. As if that were not emotional enough, the crowd of townspeople who attended the reception after the parades and wreath-layings made things even more so. Those old enough to have been present at the time of the Liberation came up to touch my wife's or my hands, to embrace us, tears in their eyes, to tell us of their joy at our arrival forty-eight years before. Their affection for America and their appreciation for the Liberation had not diminished, it had grown!

Vendôme's main square's major monument before the Nazi Occupation, as it is again today, was a metal statue of Rochambeau. The very day the Germans departed so precipitately, in any kind of vehicle they could commandeer or find, we were told, a plaster bust of Rochambeau from the local museum was put on the base where the bronze statue had stood. The pre-war original, a full figure of the Marshal, had been taken down by the Germans in January 1942 to be melted down for war use. They undoubtedly wanted to remove it as a hated reminder of the American War of Independence and the establishment of American democracy. Such an honorable spot for a defender of liberty could only recall the USA's participation in World War I and the Kaiser's defeat. The memorial remained only in the hearts and minds of liberty-loving Vendômois until well after the war was over. It was on June 5, 1974, thanks to the Cincinnati Association of France, that the original statue was replaced and inaugurated in the presence of the American ambassador, Count Michel de Rochambeau, and other officials. America and France stretched hands of friendship once more across the seas.

Presumably the French FFI had prepared our real welcome: a place for offices and to stay. A small hotel, the Hotel Saint Michel across from the bridge of the same name, had been taken over by the Germans and made their Soldatenheim, or Soldiers' Home, presumably a kind of German USO. The French owner had been summarily kicked out. Our two teams duly moved in, public rooms still decorated with German slogans and songs painted with garlands about the walls. Happily, the owner was a consummate cook who transformed our lowly C rations, either by trading or disguising, into one delicious meal after another. It was the beginning of a transformation of my tastes and a lifelong addiction to French cuisine. None of us had ever eaten so well. Canned luncheon meat worked beautifully for stuffing *tomates provençal*, and what could not be adapted easily could be bartered for fresh vegetables and products that surely did not resemble anything we had grown accustomed to in Army mess halls in the USA.

It was in the kitchen where those succulent meals were prepared that we gathered around a small radio to hear the electrifying news: Paris had been liberated! We were excited, of course, but also a bit disappointed. We had not been present at one of the war's most exhilarating moments. It was to be some time before I got to that fabled city, precisely the evening that the Germans began the infamous Battle of the Bulge. Meanwhile, we had to content ourselves with photos and descriptions. What a welcome the Americans got. If only we could have been a part of it!

Notes

1. Page 507 in Lieutenant Colonel George Dyer, formerly Combat Liaison Officer and Special Assistant to the Chief of Staff, Headquarters XII US Army Corps, Copyright by the XII Corps History association and published in Baton Rouge, LA: The Army and Navy Publishing Company, 1947, *XII Corps, Spearhead of Patton's Third Army*.

    This is now a very rare and valuable book whose writing was finished in December of 1946, close to the events the book describes.

    Official figures list July 28 as the date of XII Corps's rear echelon's move to Sartilly in Normandy, and then Le Mans on the 13th, which, as I say, is precisely when the teams I worked with spent the night in Le Mans.

2. Dyer, 156 in Chapter 8, *The Campaign for France*, 12 Aug 44–10 Sep 44.

3. Dyer, 160.

4. Dyer, 160.

5. Dyer, 160.
6. Dyer, 160.
7. Dyer, 160.
8. In 1992, with my participation, the Liberation was celebrated in St. Calais, about half-way between Le Mans and Vendôme on August 11th; in Vendôme, on August 13th, and in Blois, erroneously, as I shall point out, on August 17th, rather than the 16th when I and three comrades arrived before the chateau of Blois. Raymond Casas, in his *Les volontaires de la Liberté OU Les FFI du Loir-et-Cher (1944–1945)* has a photo taken on August 14th, p. 192, "14 août 1944, à Vendôme: La foule entoure son premier GI posant pour la posterité."

IX

THROUGHOUT THE years, then as now, people have asked me how I came to study French. I didn't think it was such a feat. After all, everybody in my school days was faced with language in some form or other. I had four and a half years of Latin, but French was another matter. My grandmother Madge was proud of her Santee ancestor, supposedly of French Huguenot descent, and a captain in our Revolutionary War. Also, right across the street from us lived a French war bride who had brought her parents to the USA. The latter spoke no English and so sat lonely and silent much of the summertime on the swing of their front porch. I began French in junior high, and hard as it was at first, I walked over to the neighbors' house and *talked*. By high school, I had an excellent teacher, who not only taught us grammar, but, miracle of miracles for that benighted age in the language arts, he even taught us to speak. By army service, I had one year of college French under my belt as well. My problem was, how could I ever afford to travel to France to put the language to use? Adolf Hitler gave me the solution.

By the time we were heading across the Channel for Utah Beach, I had convinced myself that I was prepared for anything. After all, I had been through infantry basic training as well as Air Force, I could drive a jeep, and I was ready linguistically. But it wasn't long before I had another lesson. With our new duties in France itself came some unexpected learning surprises.

In 1943, the ASTP (Army Special Training Program) at Hamilton College at Clinton, New York, had been an intensive and stimulating experience. A kind of yearbook of the program published at the college in 1944 outlines the goals and something of the methods of the program and its courses:

Most of us had taken some language courses at high school and college before coming to Hamilton, but an ASTP-taught language course is different from anything we'd ever run across before.

Previously, we'd learned perhaps to read a language; and along with that came pronunciation and hour after hour of grammar. But not so in the ASTP ... Fluency is the all-important goal.

To that end we sat in class at least two hours every day and talked. And it wasn't the instructor who did the talking either! It made no difference what we talked about. "Did you have a tough time dating that gal last weekend, soldier? Tell us about it in class – BUT IN GERMAN!" "Did you disagree with what the Professor said in Area class today? Then give us your opinion. BUT IN FRENCH!"[1]

This was the beginning of the revolution in language teaching that World War II brought about in our universities during and after the conflict. Our professors were either French or had spent considerable time in France.

95

In the field of Area, namely France and Germany, such figures as the overall-program director, Dr. Moritz J. Bonn, were also experts in their fields. The area courses were also designed for practicality rather than theory. We were even introduced to the incipient makings of the Cold War:

> Discussions in all classes of the "Area" course varied from the possibility of Russian domination of Europe to the position of the Catholic Church under the Third Republic. The purpose of the course was to foster such discussion in order that each man would acquire as broad a knowledge of Europe as possible. In summary, we feel that if we are able to find our way from the coast of Brittany to the Wilhelmstrasse and can understand the problems of race, religion, and politics which we would encounter on such a trip, our studies shall not have been in vain.[2]

Despite the excellence of Hamilton's program and the intensive and often grueling schedule at Military Intelligence's school at Camp Ritchie, Maryland, there were several things that our professors, either through ignorance or the prudery of the time, had not taught us. In those puritanical days so long before the sexual revolution had replaced longings with lust, no instructor had mentioned that bordellos were legal in France, nor did anyone think to tell us that whoremasters and madams could be one of our best sources of information. They were bursting with information about the comings and goings of Germans, collaborators, possible spies, and the like. Most of them were superpatriots to boot. Perhaps our instructors themselves were ignorant of these facts. Most of my peers and I were.

Consequently one morning as we sat obediently transcribing words being read to us aloud into phonetic symbols, the professor loudly pronounced: *phoque*. A simple French word for the mammal, seal. A word that somehow had escaped us. Its similarity to the English word for fornication, spoken in front of women teachers, unnerved us all. You can be sure that we remembered the word for seals ever after, but as none of us visited a zoo in France, the word itself ended up with limited usage.

The incredibly intensive work in phonetics was outstanding and has served me well. My favorite professors were Madame Germaine Weill, a Parisian who had found refuge in New York, and Jean Yves Dunant, an Alsatian described in the yearbook as a teacher "whose predilection for *l'air frais* forces his students to speak French with a Laplander accent." This referred to Dunant's dislike of American "overheating" to such a degree that in the face of the full fury of an upper New York State winter, we sat at class table with windows wide open. This did not diminish Dunant's popularity, however. We donned overcoats and gloves and went on speaking French.

Our teachers at both Hamilton and Ritchie had one disadvantage: they had been out of France for some time, and were therefore unaware of the realities of life under the Occupation. Their sources, of necessity, were the same newspaper and magazine articles available to everyone. The word *sinistré*, for example, was one we soon saw on signs in the streets of battered cities in Normandy. The word's similarity to "sinister" had us wondering what it meant. We came to know and to use it everywhere that there had been destruction, for it signified *victims of homelessness and destruction.*

Vendôme presented another lesson. Once into our new "Heim," we installed a desk and chair near the main entrance to the hotel. We took turns manning it to see the people coming in: who they were and what they wanted. My first visitors were a courteous middle-aged couple, the woman in a grey suit and the man in Sunday black. A soldier had forced his way into their house, demanded a bottle of champagne and that the "demoiselle" come downstairs to share it with him. To give emphasis to his demands, he had shot his rifle into a wall of the living room.

Not being sure of just what the word "demoiselle" meant in this context, and not wanting to begin my sojourn in France with offensive implications, I explained that I had not been in France very long. Would Madame mind repeating the story a bit more slowly? "Madame" did begin the story over, then with a laugh, explained: "Je sais votre problème. Nous avons une Maison de Joie": "I know your problem. We have a House of Joy." I quickly got the picture. "Demoiselle" did not mean damsel in this case, and the House of Joy was not a Chinese restaurant or an attraction in a midwestern amusement park. The "Madame" was a madam, in charge of a business ubiquitous throughout France at the time.

We contacted the MPs to ensure that there was no more violence in the Joy House. Next day, I was given a watch that had been left there, and the madam came by with one of the girls "to show off the merchandise." No wonder the French had such a reputation back home in the USA. We had expected champagne and the can-can, but this was more than suitably racy.

98

The question of race and segregation also arose while we were in Vendôme. Among the group that came nightly to the hotel to sing the *Marseillaise* there was a very attractive young woman with a parasol. One afternoon, we chatted. She asked if I was prejudiced against black people. I told her that no, I was not, that I had been brought up with black friends and thought nothing of it. She said that since so many of my compatriots were prejudiced, she wanted to be sure before inviting me to a party at the home of a local woman who was from Black Africa. I said I'd love to go with her. The hostess had a wind-up victrola, we danced, drank wine, and had a very pleasant time. No racism. Just a GI, some French guests, a beautiful girl, and a charming and cultured black hostess.

Another visit to our Soldatenheim came from two French women of the Red Cross. One, Monique de Nervo, asked if I would like to have dinner with her sister and brother-in-law who had an estate, Huchigny, nearby in the country. The next evening, we drove in my jeep to the manor house where a group of friends and family were gathered for dinner. Monique remarked on my "quaint" way of changing knife and fork when I ate, and I observed European table manners and decided that sooner or later I would acquire the skill to imitate my hosts, Hubert Jurien de la Gravière and his wife Claude de Nervo. The host was a viscount, his wife, the daughter of a baron, and her sister Monique a duchess by marriage. The amazing thing was that they all seemed quite human and down-to-earth, despite the titles. None of the snobbery an Ohioan would have expected. That night was the first time I heard talk of the fear in France of a Communist take-over.

Hubert and Claude's daughter Sylvine was a babe in

arms. A photo of us gathered together in front of the house was mailed back to Ohio. Half a century later, at a warm reunion, it is Sylvine with her husband and children who stands proudly beside her father, in the very spot where the picture had been taken in August 1944.

There was another memorable dinner in Vendôme. It was to welcome us as liberators. Many of those attending signed the menu, among them Pierre de Saint Céran, an active and much-decorated member of the Resistance and of veteran ceremonies today. The food, as Saint Céran said with humor, was all readily available on the local farms, nothing imported in those days, but copious the meal was, in food, wines, and the usual French liqueurs. The Germans didn't get everything, after all.

But not everything was jollity and feasting. We worked hard, and there was a pervading somber side to our experience in Vendôme. On one of the first days there, two distinguished men were brought in to me for questioning. They had been driving in a mail truck with a woman postal worker back to Paris from the Château d'Asnières. As they passed through Vendôme, the Germans were beginning their retreat. Lacking vehicles, they were taking anything they could find to escape our advance. The truck was commandeered, its occupants left on the sidewalk. Consequently, the two men were accused by the FFI of helping the enemy to escape. In those trigger-happy days, such an accusation could quickly result in a shooting. There was no way of communicating with Paris to verify the identity of the men, one a well-known writer and theatrical critic, Marcel Augagneur (whose pen name was Marc de Saligny) and the other, a prominent member of a Parisian engineering firm, Fernand Laurant.

Both had been imprisoned in the tower of the ancient Saint George gate where they sat and slept on straw on the floor. Fortunately, they had been sent to us, and I was able to bring about a satisfactory solution agreeable to all. A chat with the FFI and the police brought about their release from the tower to go to a small hotel. They were to sign in at the police station once a day until their story could be checked out with the proper authorities in Paris.

Not all problems were as easily solved. A lot of old scores were settled before we could intervene. In one town farther on, an Italian farm laborer was to be brought in to me to be interrogated the following morning. When I asked my FFI contact where the man was, I was told that he had been "accidentally" shot.

These were hardly heroic moments, but I did have one unique adventure: that of being the first American to set foot on the soil of the city of Blois.

Notes

1. The *ASTP Hamiltonian*. Published at Hamilton College, Clinton, New York some time after February 1944.
2. ASTP Hamiltonian, 30.

X

ANYONE WHO has been in a war knows that one characteristic of it is fluidity. We thought we were prepared for most anything, but suddenly the situation would change drastically. Stranger than fiction is the cliché, and stranger than fiction much of what we lived through was.

Hardly had we settled into the Hotel Saint Michel in Vendôme, two days after our arrival that August, when a small white *gasogène*-driven truck pulled up and delivered three collaborators. They had been brought from Blois, thirty-three kilometers or about fifteen miles to the south of us. Why these three, two men and a woman, had been brought to us was a mystery. We knew nothing about them or what they had done, whether they were dangerously pro-German and anti-American and we wondered why the American or French authorities had not taken appropriate action against them.

Major Bennett made a decision to send them back to Blois. It was late afternoon. Four of us, two from Team 443 and two from the CIC, started out in two jeeps across the stone bridge over the River Loir and headed south. I was "riding shotgun" or rather machine-gun.

The street leading into Blois, then as now, was a fairly wide one, with two-storied buildings on both sides. There

102

was not a single soul in the streets, but what we did see were tracer bullets in the lowering sky. No Americans, no French. The street led to the ancient chateau where Catherine de Medici had her secret cabinets, where her son Henry III had the Duke of Guise murdered, and where kings and princes, queens and princesses had dwelt since the Middle Ages.

The chateau loomed above us, a double staircase leading up to it. I jumped out and went up the steps. Across an open area beside the chateau I saw a man crouched. He ran over to me, pushing me to the ground and explaining that the Germans were beyond where we were and were machine-gunning the area and lobbing in mortar shells. He asked where the Americans were, not just *four* of us, but the American Army. And indeed, that is what the four of us wondered too.

The Germans had withdrawn to the other side of the Loire River that morning, but the water was low enough to wade from one side to the other, and they had a sizeable force with them, plus artillery and at least one observation plane. The FFI was understandably concerned about getting help from the Americans.

Going back to Blois in the 1990s did not initially solve the mysteries of my recollections of that night. I was correct in recalling that the space beside and beyond the terrace of the chateau was empty then, as photo documents show.[1] From the terrace, FFI members took us to the vaults lit by candles in bottles. There we were briefed on the military situation in preparation for returning to Vendôme and Army headquarters with information on the situation in and around Blois. We were told that there were possibly as many as 30,000 Germans just south of the river.

The Germans had blown up the main bridge across the Loire that morning of the 16th, and had shelled parts of the city, which explained the lack of anyone in the streets. The FFI were alert, but concerned, as were we. A return of the Germans could have resulted in a blood bath. For our part, we saw that Patton's right flank was threatened, that right flank that he so boastfully said would take care of itself and therefore should not constitute a worry. I and one of the CIC men decided to get as much information about the general situation as we could and then drive back to headquarters. We met with some of the leaders of the Resistance in a small farming village just north of the city, and got on our way, leaving two of our comrades there. Earl Coon and the other CIC man stayed on in Blois that night, giving rise to the legend that an American jeep had arrived the morning of August 17. It had been there since the evening of the 16th. We had the honor of being the first Americans. Those who came the following day were, in our opinion, Johnny-come-latelys.

We could use no headlights, of course, on our drive back, and it was very late, perhaps 0200 or more when we got to the headquarters tent.

A curious incident took place as the two of us drove along that dark road. At a crossroad, barely perceptible, we were faced with the looming hulk of a truck. We were unprepared for such an eventuality, and apparently the driver and men in the truck were as surprised as we were. They were Americans, fortunately, and equally fortunately, they did not fire on us or we on them. Naive on both parts, no doubt, but in this case luck was with us. The truck was coming from the east of our road and was hopelessly lost. Should they go south where we were coming from, they asked. We told them, no, there were only two GIs down there. There should be Americans to the west, and so they went on in that direction. We continued on, through Vendôme out to headquarters to report our startling news. We saw ourselves as the saviors of that vulnerable right flank, worthy of some kind of medal at least! We were quickly disenchanted. The officer taking down our report remained completely unruffled. He confidently reassured us. The Germans won't attack our right flank. Go get some sleep. And Patton, and the officer, of course, were right.

We were often unaware of events going on outside our immediate area of concern or responsibility. We were the first Americans in Blois, but not the first in the immediate vicinity. Histories usually call the Battle of Orleans the first one in which XII Corps was engaged, but there was another smaller battle that actually was XII's baptism by fire.

It took place near a small town named Herbault, twelve kilometers almost directly west of Blois itself, a village so tiny that some Blésois don't even know of its existence. It is, however, very clearly marked on a Michelin map as just beyond the dense forest of Blois where many Resistants took refuge. It was in the direction we had unwittingly steered the truckload of GIs on the night road to the south of Vendôme.

Dyer's XII Corps book describes the battle in some detail, giving direct accounts of what happened, explaining that it was paralleled in various skirmishes of the kind throughout France. In this case, it was the first battle experience for all of the men involved. One man from the

105

signal corps points out in the book that he and his comrades thought that the country north of the Loire was free of Germans. As they drove south, they saw no GIs, and in every town they went through, people came out, "went wild, threw flowers at us and kissed us. We were having a swell time and did not think much about it."[2]

An even greater surprise was awaiting their intrepid group, however:

> We came into the small town of Herbault, just this side of Blois. As we went through the town, we saw a man waving his arms frantically at us and jumping up and down. He had on a mixed uniform, an overseas cap with a gold bar and some civilian clothes. No one stopped as they thought he was another wild Frenchman. He finally stopped the vehicle in front of us and told the captain that the Germans had a road block ahead. It turned out he was a French-speaking American who had been dropped into France three years before by parachute.[3]

The other vehicles had gone on ahead at a fairly good clip, and so the captain was unable to reach the lead vehicle in time to stop it. The road goes through thick woods, and the lead vehicle, coming around a curve, was stopped by a road block.

> They [our GIs] were so green that they stopped and the sergeant went forward to tow it out of the way with the winch on his truck. The Germans opened up and killed both men. All the vehicles had stopped and at the rear of the column no one knew what had

happened. An order was passed back that there were Jerries in the woods and that there was a road block ahead. As if on order, you heard the safeties clank off and bolts thrown home as the men made a dash out of the vehicles and hit the ground and ditches. The engineers really were trained. They formed platoons and went into the woods. Then all hell broke loose and lead was a dime a dozen from then on.[4]

It was a "first" as well for the medics that were along with the convoy. A medical officer, Captain John Bourne, described his experience during the battle. Upon hearing firing ahead and seeing the convoy stopped, he set up a first aid station in the back of a truck. When he heard someone call for medics, he and two stretcher bearers went towards the head of the column. They were apprehensive as they had heard extensive comments that the Germans were not observing the neutral status of medical personnel that had been established by the Geneva Convention. The first man they brought back had been severely wounded in the neck. He was given plasma, but it was not possible to save him. Then a sergeant came crawling back to tell the captain about two men wounded in the lead truck. With a driver and helper in a jeep with a Red Cross flag across it, the captain drove toward the head of the column, and as he did so, he raised his hand. This was interpreted as a sign to cease firing, which first the Americans and then the Germans did. A shell burst overhead, the captain admitted his fright, but he saw to it that the injured men were driven out several minutes before the battle resumed.

The convoy was there about five hours, but once it was clear that the Germans outnumbered and outgunned our men, and had heavy artillery as well, the decision was made to withdraw. Local FFI men drew from memory a detailed map of all the German installations in the area and led the exhausted men back to Herbault where people gave them some wine to recover their spirits.

The first XII Corps battle was at an end. It may have been rumors about this fighting that were interpreted as our having been surrounded in Vendôme. A better case, obviously, could have been made for Blois.

Resistance veteran and historian Raymond Casas of Blois feels certain that the meeting on the evening of our arrival took place in an underground portion of the chateau, by the façade of the wing build by King Louis XII. I am more inclined to think that the place was the basement of the current Hotel Ibis, which had been the German Kommandantur, and which is about half a block below the chateau.

At any rate, the person with whom we made contact was, according to Casas, a member of the FFI whose name was Auguste Lebon. He held the rank of lieutenant and had had a long and distinguished record of combat, first in Morocco, then as a volunteer in the Spanish Civil War where he was wounded several times. He was also gravely wounded in the fighting of 1940. Made prisoner by the Germans, he refused to go to work in Germany and was sent to a salt mine in Silesia. Repatriated for health reasons, he immediately joined the underground and was cited for his courage and heroism. He was killed during a mission on August 24, 1944.[5]

It was not Casas, however, but another member of the Resistance who came up to me at the reception following the official Liberation ceremonies in Blois on August 17,

1992, and said quite simply, "J'étais là," "I was there." He did indeed remember meeting me and my GI companions on the night of the 16th, 1944, but it was not on the terrace of the chateau where earlier that night I had had my first contact with the FFI. We two had met later in the night at a farm on the edges of a village just north of the city before our departure for Vendôme.

The man's name was Jean Deck, a gentle, warm, and dignified man, by profession an electrician, who joined the Resistance at the age of 17. He became a member of one of the first and most respected Resistance units in all of France, the *Réseau Musée de l'Homme* (Network of the Museum of Man), at the Palais de Chaillot just across the Seine from the Eiffel Tower. Some of France's most highly respected intellectuals were administrators there and joined the network one month after France's fall to the Nazis.

Jean Deck has written two accounts for this book, one concerning the group he joined in 1940, and the other to describe the events of August 16th and his meeting with the four first Americans to arrive in Blois. His words eloquently outline the beginnings of Resistance to the German occupiers:

The armistice of June 1940 and the German occupation of the northern zone of France provoked an immediate reaction in certain Frenchmen (about 2%). I had the honor to be among them. We refused to accept the defeat, the vexations of the occupier and his constraints. We refused also to recognize the abolition of the Republic by the reactionary Pétain and his Fascist-leaning French State.

109

Some embryos of the *Réseau* were created as early as July 1940. I think everything began with a student manifestation on the Champs-Elysées the day of July 14 1940 (Bastille Day) which was severely suppressed. It was at that time that Charles Tillion created the movement of the *Franc Tireurs et Partisans* [Irregulars and Partisans] which was to be one of the principal components of the Resistance for the next four years. The *Réseau du Musée de l'Homme* was born at the same time.

The latter was formed, as its name indicates, at the Museum of Man at the Palais de Chaillot in Paris. It was there that a group of scholars and university students decided to combat a fait accompli, and to do so by all possible means. Among the members were Paul Houet and Boris Vildé – the founders – Pierre Brosselette, Postel Vinay, Madame Desroches-Noblecourt (the Egyptologist) Anatole Lewitsky, Germaine Tillion who took over the direction, and many others.[6]

Deck tells of his parents, republican in their very beings, who had instilled in him the value and love of liberty. A close friend, Pierre Dessinges, then a student in Paris, had been asked to form a Resistance group in the Blois area. That was how the unit known as *France-Liberté* came into being in November 1940.

Its activities were varied: to combat the occupier and Vichy, to become part of the nascent resistance movements, to distribute tracts, letters, and posters, to gather up arms left from the defeat as well as to steal German arms with a view to future actions, to help the Allies however possible, including the hiding of Allied aviators parachuting into France, to help the Jews already sensing repressions to come, to carry communications between the Free and Occupied zones, to sabotage transportation, to fabricate false identification papers, to help escaped prisoners to cross the Cher River into the Unoccupied Zone and to hide any of the latter if passage had to be postponed.

A French priest "sold" the group to the Gestapo. German police infiltrated the group, resulting in numbers of arrests, with the resultant torture, imprisonment and deaths. Deck escaped and went on to join the British Special Operations Executive (SOE) group called Prosper and a group known as Buckminster. Working for the British, Deck says, did not carry the prestige of working with the Americans, interestingly enough.

The parachuting of agents from Britain became particularly important in the region to the south of Blois. Casas gives a listing of sixty-four aviators and agents dropped into the Loir et Cher area from 1942 until 1944.[7] Wooded hills and small rivers and streams made this particular area compatible with underground activities as people could hide out over periods of time when and if necessary.

The River Cher being the crossing point between the occupied and Vichy zones of France made this a very attractive area for those trying to flee Nazi repression. The small city of Selles-sur-Cher directly south of Blois was a central checkpoint between the zones. Not far to the south of it, on the outskirts of Valençay, best known for its imposing chateau that once belonged to the talented diplomat, sybarite and lecher, Talleyrand, stands a strange-looking monument. It is a metal column with a circular

111

disk in its upper center and commemorates the night of May 5–6, 1941 when the first secret agent was dropped onto French soil. It was dedicated in May 1991 by Britain's Queen Mother.

As the monument's marker points out, Churchill had begun the SOE for the purpose of promoting resistance, sabotage and subversion. The first agent was a radio operator named Georges Begue who made contact with a local man, Max Hymans. He was to be followed in various parts of the country by some four hundred other agents. The monument is also dedicated to the *Reseau Buckminster* to which Jean Deck belonged after the German arrest of the *Reseau Musée de l'Homme*.

In his letter to me describing the day and evening of August 16, 1944, Deck gives a graphic depiction of what was Blois's last day of German occupation.

Dear Friend:

During a telephone conversation, Monsieur Couppé just told me of your wish to have me give you as detailed an account as possible of the events that took place in Blois on August 16, 1944, as far as I personally was involved. I recount them to you as well as I can as I dig into memories that are now 48 years old. I became a member of a network of *France combattante* in December 1940 when I was 17 years old. After passing through several organizations, including the English SOE, I finished my participation in the Resistance at the age of 20 and a half as the liaison and information agent for Colonel de la Vaissière – alias Valin – who was the head of the *département* [Loir et Cher] Unified Forces of the [French] Resistance.

No need to tell you what memories I have of that extraordinary but dangerous period. Many of my comrades gave their lives, but it was my [good] luck to pass through the loopholes in their traps. I still have a certain nostalgia for that period, not for the horrors of the Occupation, but for all the human relationships that it was possible for me to have at that time. It was a marvelous experience for a young person like myself who was on the threshold of an active life.

On the afternoon of August 15, 1944, Colonel de la Vaissière, my leader in the Resistance whose agent I was for liaison and information for the southern part of Loir et Cher, sent me to Jouy le Potier to a certain farm where I was to meet Colonel Dufour, one of the heads of the Resistance that formed part of the BCRA of General de Gaulle, so that I could negotiate his integration into the departmental Resistance forces, and to set up a meeting to that effect.

On my return early in the afternoon of August 16, so that I could avoid using the bridge at Blois, always dangerous due to German patrols, I went to cross the Loire by boat at Rilly-sur-Loire, fifteen kilometers downstream from Blois, with the help of a local ferry man in the Resistance.

I went back following the road that ran along the banks of the river and, on getting to Blois in the early afternoon, I heard unexpected noises of shooting, mortar shots, etc. As I walked up the slope of the Boulevard Daniel Dupuis to the meeting that had been set up, I looked down toward the Loire and the city below me. Then I heard an enormous explosion and I saw the bridge of Blois blow up.

I understood immediately that under the pressure of the forces of the Resistance, the Germans had left the northern part of the city (the most important part). The shooting continued on both sides of the river.

At my meeting, I learned that Colonel Valin was at a get-together at the Trois Marchants Hotel at Herbaut to the north of Blois. Another comrade, who like me was an agent for liaison, Maurice Guiou whom I had just run into, said he would accompany me and as we wanted to get as much information as we could, we went by the Prefecture. There, a group of non-coms in the Resistance with whom I was acquainted were having a discussion with a man in civilian clothes whom I did not know. They asked us where to find the Colonel.

Once it was clear that we were on our way to find him, the man in civilian clothes told us that he was the new Prefect of the *département*. He scratched out a little note which he gave us to take to the Colonel and which was worded in English as follows: "The town is free."

On arrival at Herbaut, we met with the Colonel who, among others, was accompanied by Monsieur Lucien Jardel – a friend of mine – who was President of the Loir et Cher Committee for the Liberation.

Curiously enough, shortly after that, another liaison agent whom I did not know, came up also with the same missive. A lack of confidence, no doubt? Lucien Jardel was also the head of one of the Resistance groups that had been active that day in Blois. At the request of the Colonel who had set a meeting with us for the next morning at the Prefecture of Blois, and also so that we could ascertain what had actually happened, Maurice Guiou and I left in a car with Lucien Jardel who wanted to rejoin his unit in the northern sector of the city of Blois.

We drove to Villebarou, a village on the road to Vendôme. In a small farm there, a group of Resistance fighters of those who had participated in the "clean-up" operations of the city, were quite "gay," very excited and were celebrating the event.

We ate a meal there and, at about 11 or 12 o'clock at night, before stretching out to go to sleep, we were surprised to see two American soldiers walk in. They had arrived in two jeeps which were under guard by two of their colleagues.

Those two GIs said they were coming back from a reconnaissance in a deserted Blois, and were searching for information about the state of the German troops in the area. They told us that they were part of a unit in the vanguard of the information service of Patton's Army, that they had come from Vendôme and were going back there.

As Maurice and I regularly covered the area of the southern part of the *département*, we informed them as well as we could. After a warm handshake, they left.

I remember this episode with complete clarity as these were the first American soldiers I had seen or talked with. I always wondered how they got to where we were.

At that time, the towns and farms had a "blackout," and people holed up at home as soon as night fell. In the euphoria of that night, the lights of the courtyard and of the house shone brightly and were visible from far off. Could they have been attracted [to us] by the lights? That is really a very strange set of circumstances!

That is roughly the tale of the evening of August 16, 1944. The question that is raised is to know if it was you. That would be marvelous! On the one hand, it is most improbable that there would be four other GIs except for you who would have carried out the same mission at the same place on the same day. Can you find an answer to this enigma? I hope so and that it really was you.

I forgot a detail. One of the two American soldiers spoke French, a French that was slightly halting, but good all the same.

When I went to that ceremony at the City Hall of Blois to which I had been invited, I had absolutely no idea of meeting you again. After I had heard the speeches, I recalled this episode, and that is when my friend Lemire introduced me to you.

The two GIs who spoke French were Master Sergeant Earl O. Coon and myself. I had the better accent of the two. My closest CIC buddy, Ralph Palmer, believes the two CIC men we were with were Bud Hock (William G.) and Gale Hart, the former from Covington, Kentucky, and the latter from New Mexico. We had forgotten the collaborationists, and no record of them seems to exist.

That same day, August 16th, XII Corps captured Orleans, the important communications center directly south of Paris on the Loire. Some of our "team" had gone into

Orleans ahead of the lead tanks. The guys came back unscathed but grumbling that they had been the expendables for the armored vehicles. And naturally, as Patton's Third advanced on to the north-east, our men moved on too. As I had made some acquaintances in Vendôme, it was decided that I would stay on a couple of days. That was how I happened to be there when the news came over the radio that Paris had been freed on August 24 and 25.

Notes

1. Christian Couppé's book *Blois des bombes et ruines 1940–1944* shows ample evidence of the 1940 destruction of most of the section from the chateau going to the river. The area was just one large empty lot, without a single building or dwelling surviving. The area was, however, rebuilt in the post-war period and consequently looks quite different now.
2. Dyer, 170. The soldier describing this part of the event was T/5 Frank C. Nodine of the 93rd Signal Battalion that was to cut German telephone wires while our American engineers blew up the Loire River bridges.
3. Dyer, 170.
4. Dyer, 170.
5. The information re Lebon comes from the funeral oration pronounced by another important Resistance figure, Major Judes, whose code name was Richard, and reproduced in Casas's book, *Les volontaires de la Liberté*.
6. The translation is my own. The letter is dated January 19, 1994.
7. In his *Les volontaires de la Liberté*.

XI

THE RESISTANCE MEN we met in Blois that night in 1944 could stand proud for their heroism. Their stories still fascinate and impress after half a century. They had risked their necks and those of their families and friends to fight the occupier of their native land and to work with us. They had participated in rescuing Allied airmen, in blowing up bridges and rail lines, in cutting telephone lines, and all the rest.

Knowing all that, and given our enthusiastic welcome in Normandy and cities like Vendôme, it seemed that France was unified in its joy at being liberated. But like it or not, there was that dark side of a France that had collaborated with the enemy, whether for greed, self-aggrandisement or through political conviction. There were French Fascists and their adherents. The France we found ourselves in had been, and in some ways remained, deeply divided ideologically. Ugly things had gone on.

One thorny question was the legitimacy of a French government. Who was the official administrator of France? The Pétain government had been recognized by the United States in 1940. Initially, the Americans admired Pétain and offered him support. The Germans were victorious in France, and the Vichy government had taken over.

The Vichy regime appeared to the Americans to be the legitimate successor to the Third Republic and they did not hesitate to recognize it. To a certain extent, the fact that a regime had been established at Vichy which seemed to have some marginal independence from the Germans was rather more than Roosevelt could have hoped for after the gloomy first dispatches of his ambassador in France. The Americans made clear to Pétain that they admired him and were willing to offer him support, but only on condition that the French fleet did not fall into German hands, that French North Africa and other colonies remained under Vichy control, and that the regime afforded no aid to the German war effort against Britain. In support of this policy, the American government was willing to give material aid to Vichy as a means of assuaging its worst subsistence problems, so that it might retain the loyalty of the people and be in a position to resist German demands for greater collaboration.[1]

A meeting of Pétain with Hitler in Montoire and the return of Laval to power invalidated our policy, but recognition of Vichy by the Americans was by no means a minor matter. Serious damage was done to de Gaulle and to his Free French. Who, after all, was this de Gaulle? And Pétain? He was, after all, a revered hero of the First World War barely over two decades earlier. Moreover, he espoused basic values most of the French people shared, a love of home, family, and the *patrie*. He represented a kind of stability after all the pre-war years of political turmoil, the war itself, the crushing defeat and the collapse of both army and government. Loyalty and patriotism were important to every French man and woman. The battle for the mind and soul of France was a fierce one. Pétain and Vichy? De Gaulle? Churchill and the Allies? Germany and Fascism?

The BBC undertook its "psychological warfare" of transmitting information and intelligence as early as July 1940. In 1941, Churchill created the Political Warfare Executive, whose mission was to sustain and encourage resistance movements in the occupied countries.

The Germans were well prepared too. Goebbels' Propaganda Ministry in Berlin had proven its abilities within Germany's own borders. It quickly went into action in metropolitan France, and met with significant success in many quarters. While we on our side were bombarded with tales of German savagery and destruction of all civilized values, Goebbels' competent minions were saying much the same sort of thing, attacking us and the British as the ravagers of Europe's cultural heritage. Germany was portrayed as the defender of Europe against the Bolsheviks, as well as the rampant capitalism of the United States. Allied bombing, whose results could be seen and felt throughout France, was described as barbarous and indiscriminate. Also Germany was always portrayed as the eventual victor in the war, another point that affected people's attitudes towards the resistance or collaboration.

By the time of the invasion and our two-month battle for the Cotentin area, France had undergone four years of occupation and propaganda assault. All media were under strict control. Such prestigious pre-war magazines as *Illustration*, probably the most handsome publication of its kind ever, or *Match*, were completely under the domination of the Occupation authorities. Front covers featured the grandfatherly Marshal Pétain talking with villagers, victorious German troops facing the Bolshevik enemy, and the like. Posters, often of excellent design, brought political messages home to the French public on street after street, and the most virulent anti-Semitic caricatures spewed Jew-hatred with considerable effectiveness. Dialogue and overt dissension were a thing of the past, but clandestine publications did grow in number as German repression gained in ferocity.

Be it said that Pétain did try to salvage something from the bitter ashes of defeat. Hitler met Pétain on October 24, 1940, in the railroad station of Montoire, not far from Vendôme, a site chosen because a tunnel nearby offered the Fuhrer's train protection against air attack. The meeting is one that is still hotly debated. To many, the handshake of the Marshal with the Reich's Chancellor was open treachery; to others it was an attempt to wrest concessions for the benefit of France, the release of some two million Frenchmen being held prisoner in Germany, a lowering of reparations, and a relaxation of control at the demarcation line between so-called free Vichy France and the openly occupied regions of the north and the coastal areas. France was divided geographically and would become more and more so ideologically.

At first, the French were staggered by the military might of the victors. German soldiers were given orders to present a friendly face to their terrified new vassals. Posters went up showing them smiling, hands outstretched in friendship. It was the beginning of the battle to numb the French spirit, abetted by the French Right.

One of the major figures of that Right was the writer, the aged Charles Maurras, who saw in Pétain the only hope for maintaining any kind of national integrity. A few days after the meeting at Montoire, Maurras wrote:

France's greatest misfortune would be if people were to take sides over "collaboration" and form opposing factions. This dispersion and diversion would be fatal. Everything should lead to inconclusion and concentration.

The Marshal is responsible. He expressed it admirably. Let us understand...

"But if..."

"There is no if. First concentration. We must think of *France, France alone*... It is for her we must work."

So our mission is to fortify the pivot on which everything rolls and turns, without questioning the political tendency.[2]

Other younger writers like Robert Brasillach, who was executed as a traitor in Paris in 1945, shared Maurras' views. As we read his work, we can see how divisive French pre-war politics had been, and what the impact of the defeat and armistice of 1940 meant to him:

We forget what the Armistice then meant for a country about to be condemned, lost, invaded from end to end, where shelters were being dug before the *Prefecture* of Perpignan [near the Spanish border]. We forget the human lives which this act had saved, the children who could breathe again, the millions of people who could once more look up at a harmless sky no longer filled with murderous lead.[3]

Brasillach wrote that in June 1941. In October he wrote as tellingly about the feelings of many Frenchmen living in a conquered nation:

Every Frenchman will have understood that each time the much jeopardized Franco-German reconciliation is about to be proclaimed, London, supported by Moscow, gets in the way. Each time there is talk of negotiations and hope of a new return of prisoners, our plans are upset by elements which *on no account* want the survival and welfare of France.

Do you want our comrades, more than a million men of under forty, to stay behind the barbed wire of prison camps for months and years, so that there should be no danger of their supporting a hostile country?

Do you want France, bereft of a large part of her territory and empire, to become a vague subprovince of greater Europe?

Do you want every day of next winter to be harder for you? Do you want your life disrupted at every moment because of this state of emergency? Don't you want anybody, for any reason, however serious, to be allowed in the street between dusk and dawn?

Do you want your children brought up in fear and misery, with no future but to become laborers and mercenaries?[4]

Ironically, much of what Brasillach says here to justify

support for Vichy and collaboration are the very reasons for active resistance. France had become a kind of province, many people were being reduced to the level of laborers, and her moral and material suffering became increasingly greater the longer the war went on.

No true Frenchman could consider the Germans as legitimate officials of France, but if Pétain and his henchmen were not the lawful government, who was? The resulting ambivalence was further exacerbated by President Franklin D. Roosevelt's attitude and his unswerving hostility to General de Gaulle. As D-Day came ever closer, it was apparent to military leaders, and particularly Eisenhower, that a clear decision to recognize de Gaulle as the legitimate head of France was imperative. Only he could rally the support of the Resistance, of such importance to helping the Allies.[5]

Roosevelt's antipathy to de Gaulle was shared to a degree by Churchill. Both leaders found their French counterpart at best a prickly and stubborn ally. Churchill had been willing to recognize de Gaulle as head of the Free French, but Roosevelt refused. Churchill did at least comprehend de Gaulle's position and even his arrogance vis-à-vis the Allies "to prove to French eyes that he was not a British puppet." Churchill even expressed admiration for de Gaulle's "massive strength."[6]

Roosevelt's candidate to represent Free France had been General Henri Giraud. André Malraux, heroic Resistance fighter, noted author and Minister of Culture under de Gaulle in post-war France, described Giraud as: "A gallant soldier who was as well fitted to undertake the difficult burden of the liberation of France as I am to be a Chinese actor."[7] At the Casablanca conference in 1943, however, a show of national unity between Giraud and de Gaulle was important. Churchill recognized this. He had singular problems persuading the latter to attend, however. Some of the repartee over this is witty, despite the seriousness of the situation:

At the Casablanca conference with Churchill, Roosevelt saw the dramatic need for a show of unity between de Gaulle and Giraud and told Churchill: "You bring the bride and I'll bring the bridegroom." But embittered de Gaulle refused and FDR teased Churchill about his "bad boy" who played Joan of Arc, and Churchill reportedly said: "Yes, but my bloody bishops won't let me burn him."[8]

It was only when Churchill threatened to cut off all supplies and support that de Gaulle reneged and attended the conference where he had a stormy private meeting with FDR, and posed shaking hands with Giraud. Vichy had long before condemned de Gaulle to death *in absentia*, and many matters and people were affected by all of this.

There was also a lengthy struggle over whether French or Allied military authorities would be in charge on French soil after the invasion. This was a matter of extreme importance in dealing with local officials as large numbers of American troops moved into France. Who was to be obeyed? SHAEF's waffling resulted in muddying a lot of waters, for the French populace first, but also for us in the Intelligence service. Both civil and military authorities suffered the consequences.

Jacques Kayser, the French journalist whose journals were published posthumously by his son,[9] is a case in point. Officially a member of de Gaulle's Free French forces and very highly placed, Kayser had to battle his way over a whole series of bureaucratic politico-administrative barriers before getting permission to go into Normandy. He finally crossed the Channel on June 30th, and even then had to wait until July 14th until SHAEF in London accredited him as Public Relations Officer. Two days later, SHAEF in Normandy introduced Kayser to the officer in charge of public relations for the American, British and Canadian armies.

Add these frustrations to the concerns Kayser had on going back to his native France where he found "skin-deep sensitivities, mental instability, contradictions, ambivalence, fears, dispassion..."[10] A gap of considerable proportions between officers of the Free French who had been living outside France and those of the Forces Françaises of the Interior [FFI] was something that not only Kayser had to deal with. So did those of us working directly with the French on a daily basis. And there was the question of Allied bombardments. What was their effect on public opinion? Further Kayser noted early on the concerns related to the denunciations and purges of various kinds of collaborators.

The Germans were fully aware of the dissensions in France and exploited them. Anti-Semitic propaganda was brutal and often very effective. Preying on the persisting tendency in French life and politics towards xenophobia, Vichy racial laws stemmed very clearly from Vichy policy and were not, as often asserted in the post-war Liberation purges, initiated and imposed by the Occupation authorities. Within twelve days after Pétain's investiture as Head of State, a commission was set up to review the naturalization of recent immigrants to France, as a result of which 15,000 citizens had their status revoked. Of that number, some 6000 were Jewish, in effect condemning them to deportation and death.[11] The story of the Jews in France during the Occupation is not one for France in general to be proud of, but here again, there were acts of self-sacrifice and heroism along with the callous treatment meted out by Vichy officials and members of the Milice. France had been a leader in enlightened policies toward the Jews, but anti-Semitism was also deeply rooted in large segments of French Catholic society and had been for centuries. The Germans did an effective job of establishing the Jew as the supporter of Godless Bolshevism and as the anti-Christ. The Crusade against Communism was also a crusade against the Jew, the perennial scapegoat.

Notes

1. In Hilary Footitt and John Simmonds' *France 1943–1945.* New York: Holmes and Meier, 1988. The Politics of Liberation Series, 11.
2. In Germaine Brée and George Bernauer's *Defeat and Beyond, An Anthology of French Wartime Writing, 1940–1945.* New York: Pantheon Books, 1970, 97–8. This excellent book makes a fine introduction for anyone interested in reading these French sources in translation, guided by Ms. Brée's skilled, balanced and insightful introductory materials. There is also an excellent bibliography of books primarily in French, and a bibliographical glossary of writers and figures in France in the Occupation and Liberation periods.
3. Brée-Bernauer, *Defeat,* 238.
4. Brée-Bernauer, *Defeat,* 238–9.
5. A clear succinct discussion of the American politics of the pre-invasion years is given in Hilary Footitt and John Simmonds'

France 1943–1945, in The Politics of Liberation Series, New York: Holmes and Meier, 1988.

6. In Richard Harrity and Ralph G. Martin's *Man of Destiny, De Gaulle of France*. New York: Duell, Sloan and Pearce, 1961, 93.
7. *Man of Destiny*, 95.
8. *Man of Destiny*, 96.
9. See Chapter 5, Footitt and Simmonds.
10. In Kayser, 12–13.
11. Information in this section is based primarily on Michael R. Marrus and Robert O. Paxton, *Vichy France and the Jews*. New York: Schocken Books, 1983, and on the brief but excellent interview with Paxton published as a special section of *Le Figaro*, 13 août, 1990 in a series entitled "Il y a cinquante ans: L'année 1940."

Above: General George S. Patton Jr.

Right: With Helen Patton, Avranches, 31 July, 1994

Below: Christian Couppé with mother Georgina Patton, the general's granddaughter at Néhou, June 3, 1994.

Right: The author holding Nicole Chenais beside Guy Chenais in St. Calais, France, August 14 1944.

Right: The author at St. Calais with Nicole Chenais Blu and her brother Guy Chenais, fifty years later.

Above: The day before Christmas, 1944, Luxembourg.

Above: Luxembourg, 1993.

Right: Mayor of Maillé and Christian Couppé,
August 28, 1994.

Bottom: Liberation ceremonies at Blois,
September 7, 1994.

Below: Maillé cemetery France,
August 28, 1994.

Above: Utah Beach, Normandy, June 7, 1994 with Christian Couppé and his son Bertrand.

Above: Before the home of Claude Grenier, Châlons, April 19, 1993.

Above: Return to Néhou, August 7, 1994.

Above: Christian Couppé, Hugh Harter, Frances Harter, 31 July 1994.

Right: Team 443 listing.

Par 5, SO 135, WD MITC, 6 June 1944. (Contd)

Rank	Name	A.S.N.	A/S	SSN	Team Position

Team No 115

2D LT	EDMUND C. JANN	01317088	INF	9316	Officer in Charge
2D LT	HERMAN L. LANG	01326099	INF	9316	Interrogator
M Sgt	ERNEST WALLACH	35144719		631	Asst Interrogator
S Sgt	JOHN W. MANNHEIM	36612459		631	Document Examiner
Tec 3	BURTON HASTINGS	32780686		631	Typist Linguist
Tec 5	HENRY BUTLER	32784253		631	Chauffeur

MI INTERPRETER TEAMS (FRENCH)

Team No 116

2D LT	HENRY R. HAMMOND	01042043	CAC	9332	Officer in Charge
2D LT	ROLF C. AFGER	01325824	INF	9332	Interpreter
M Sgt	EARL O. COON	32141821		631	Asst Interpreter
S Sgt	AUDACE PREVITI	32174952		631	Translator
Tec 3	CHARLES H. JENNINGS, JR	39911015		631	Typist Linguist
Tec 3	HUGH A. HARTER	35621396		631	Typist Linguist

Team No 117

CAPT	EDGAR A. ESCHMANN, JR	0452438	INF	9332	Officer in Charge
2D LT	ROBERT I. WECHSLER	01062097	CAC	9332	Interpreter
M Sgt	THOMAS DOLOFF	42038498		631	Asst Interpreter
S Sgt	CLARENCE W. FREEMAN, JR	32261789		631	Translator
Tec 3	BERNARD ROSEN	32637757		631	Typist Linguist
Tec 3	ABRAM MASON	42045529		631	Typist Linguist

MI INTERPRETER TEAM (FLEMISH)

Team No 118

2D LT	FELIX R. FREUDMANN	01181825	FA	9332	Officer in Charge
2D LT	FRANK R. BINGHAM	01325812	INF	9332	Interpreter
M Sgt	GERRIT J. HEYNEKER	32525715		631	Asst Interpreter
S Sgt	HAROLD LEEDS	39090742		631	Translator
Tec 3	JACQUES L. GODSCHALK	32496205		631	Typist Linguist
Tec 3	HENRY S. REESE	32430025		631	Typist Linguist

ORDER OF BATTLE TEAMS

Team No 119

2D LT	IRWIN WINER	01047846	CAC	9318	Officer in Charge
M Sgt	FRED L. TUTEUR	32932010		631	Order of Battle Analyst
S Sgt	SIEGFRIED M. KRAMER	32524747		631	Order of Battle Analyst

Team No 120

1ST LT	JAMES W. BAKER	01049722	CAC	9318	Officer in Charge
M Sgt	JOHN F. KRASNY	34170536		631	Order of Battle Analyst
S Sgt	JACQUES W. KASMAN	32827511		631	Order of Battle Analyst

Above: Saint Calais for Liberation ceremonies, August 13, 1994.

Left: Vendôme, Liberation ceremonies, August 13, 1994 with Resistance Leader Pierre de Saint Céran and his wife.

Left: Vendôme, Liberation ceremonies 1992, with Paul Dujardin and Paul Huser.

Right: The author on arrival in Vendôme, France, August 14, 1944.

Right: Vendôme, The Place Saint Martin fifty years later.

Left: In front of the Chateau of Blois here the author arrived the evening of August 16, 1944, here with Christian Couppé of Blois.

Below: Daniel Chanet, Mayor of Vendôme at ceremonies on, August 12, 1994.

Below: Ceremonies at Ouzouer-le-Marché, August 15, 1994.

Right: July 31, 1994 celebration the liberation of Arranches.

Below: The present "Place Patton" in Avranches as it was after the fighting in late July, early August, 1944.

Above: Place Patton, Arranches, August 1993.

Below: Military Intelligence Team 443.

Above: A luncheon reunion in Boston with the Bretons and Palmers, May 10, 1993.

Above: Réne Marin with his wife, August 1994.

Left: Return to Sens, the Hotel de Paris et La Poste.

Above: Paule and Emile (Mimi) Gallien, police inspector in Dombasle in 1944.

Above: Michel Hachet of the Toul museum before the home of Dr. Rhotan, April 22, 1993.

Above: Hubert Payon, Resistance leader in Nancy in 1944, with wife Mimi, 1993.

Right: With Jean Deck and Georges Fabre, members of the French Resistance who 'met' Harter on August 16, 1994 in Blois.

Below: Odette Schneider of Dombasle, a friend who remembered the author's stay in 1944.

Above: The stairway up to the office used by Harter and Ralph Palmer (CIC) in Dombasle, 21 April, 1993.

Above: Resistance leader Jean Césard, Dombasle, April 21, 1993.

Above: Before the Hotel de Ville, Nancy where intelligence unit had its offices in 1994.

Above: The author on a return to Nancy, with Emile Gallien, police inspector in Dombasle (Louraine) in 1944, with Madame Paule Gallien.

Above: Bastogne, Belgium, beside a tank from the Fourth Armoured Division of Third Army and a marker on the "Route of Liberty" in the foreground.

Above: Near the artillery implacement visited on December 13, 1944.

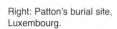

Right: Patton's burial site, Luxembourg.

XII

THERE ARE RECORDS of Jews in France as early as the time of Augustus Caesar. Their history is the usual one for Western Europe, the forced conversions, the choice of the sword or the cross, the moments of prominence and royal favor alternating with repression and massacre. Nevertheless, when compared with the rigors of the Inquisition in Spain, France seems relatively liberal, and Spanish *conversos* crossed the border to reside in France. With the Enlightenment in the eighteenth century, attitudes and comportment toward the Jews underwent a change for the better. France was in the forefront of European nations.

The first edict affecting the Jews favorably came from none other than that much maligned but surprisingly enlightened monarch, Louis XVI. A "body tax" was abolished in 1784, and the king's minister, Malesherbes, was instructed to prepare legislation establishing civil rights for Protestants, to be followed by the same for the Jewish population. The Revolution did even more. In 1790 and 1791 the Jews were given the status of French citizens,[1] but Napoleon issued restrictive decrees that affected both the Jews' civil status and their economic gains. With the restoration of the monarchy, however, the

Jews made steady progress in gaining rights. The nineteenth century saw major changes, and ended with the opening of careers in almost every field, including the army. But anti-Semitism lingered in the background.

In 1894, it exploded with the arrest and trial of Captain Alfred Dreyfus, his condemnation, imprisonment, and subsequent vindication in 1905. France was deeply divided over the case, and scars were left, to be resuscitated only with the election of the Socialist Leon Blum as premier in the mid-nineteen thirties. By then, large numbers of "foreign" Jews had come to France, primarily from the countries of Eastern Europe. With the arrival of the Nazis in 1940, those Jews were the first target of propaganda and were marked for destruction.

By August and September of 1940, laws had been passed effectively eliminating Jews from the professions. From then on, they could be practiced only by those born "of a French father." The persecution and the active collusion with the Germans in deportations increased as the war went on and lasted until the Liberation:

> During the four years it ruled from Vichy, in the shadow of Nazism, the French government energetically persecuted Jews living in France. Persecution began in the summer of 1940 when the Vichy regime, born of defeat at the hands of the Nazis and of a policy of collaboration urged by many Frenchmen, introduced a series of anti-Semitic measures. After defining who was by law a Jew, and excluding Jews from various private and public spheres of life, Vichy imposed specifically discriminatory measures: confiscating property belonging to Jews, restricting their

movements, and interning many Jews in special camps. Then, during the summer of 1942, the Germans, on their side, began to implement the "final solution" of the Jewish problem in France. Arrest, internments, and deportations to Auschwitz in Poland occurred with increasing frequency, often with the direct complicity of the French government and administration. Ultimately, close to seventy-six thousand Jews left France in cattle cars – "to the East," the Germans said: of these Jews only about 3 percent returned at the end of the war.[2]

A yellow Star of David had to be worn by all Jews. Signs in restaurant windows proclaimed, in French and in German, that entry was forbidden to Jews, as it was to cafés, theaters, movie houses, concert and music halls, markets and fairs, museums and libraries, sporting events, and public parks. Even the use of public telephones was denied them. Any change of address had to be reported, and after 1942, the word *Juif* had to appear on ration and identity cards. Only the last car in the Métro could be utilized by Jews. Shopping was restricted to the afternoon, when hardly anything was left to buy.

Far worse than that, however, were the *camps de concentration* that contributed one of the darkest chapters in Vichy policy toward the Jews, and were responsible for several thousand deaths in France – mostly of Jews, but also of gypsies and other political prisoners such as veterans of the international brigades in Spain.

This part of the anti-Jewish system involved few

ordinary French citizens and, indeed, only a narrow sector of the French administration. But it was one in which a combination of scarcity and callousness produced horrors and suffering to a degree that shocked French and foreign opinion when the truth began to leak out...[3]

The roundups of Jews and their deportation grew in volume. The most notorious was that of July 1942 when 12,884 Jewish men and women and more than 4000 children were taken to the sports arena known as the Val d'Hiver, where conditions were horrifying. Most of the arrests were made by French police, assisted by blue-shirted followers of super-collaborator Jacques Doriot. After five days of confinement, the inmates were moved to the infamous camp at Drancy from which they were then shipped off to Auschwitz for extermination. When Drancy was finally liberated in August 1944, there were still 1500 Jews confined there. The last shipment had gone out on July 31st, to make a total of over 75,000 deported from French soil. The police followed orders, but to the credit of some, they did warn those about to be arrested in time for them to escape. Public opinion became increasingly outraged as knowledge of what was happening became widely known.

In French North Africa, Algeria, Morocco, and Tunisia, there was a large Jewish population affected by the racial laws which, incredibly enough, remained in force well after the Allies had driven the Germans and Vichy officials out. This was with the explicit approval of General Giraud, FDR's preferred candidate to be the head of a new French government. Still more shocking was Roosevelt's declaration to General Auguste Nogues, a Vichy administrator who had turned coat by the time of the Casablanca conference, that proposed quotas on Jews entering professions were comprehensible, representing, as they did a "small part" of the population, while, in Germany itself, they had compromised almost fifty percent of the lawyers, doctors, teachers and professions.[4]

In this, as in the official recognition of Vichy, the American government clearly muddied the waters of French politics, lending strength to some of the most reactionary elements in France. Gentiles were increasingly threatened if they attempted to help Jews in any way, but more and more people and groups ran the risk. As the mass deportations increased, so did the aid of Resistance cadres. Nevertheless, the Jewish "problem" seems to have evoked relatively little concern from the majority of Frenchmen for whom "other matters – the future of France, an absent husband or son, the next meal – occupied the attention of many."[5]

As the Resistance movement grew, Jewish participants grew in ever increasing numbers, and the Jewish persecution came to be perceived more and more as a part of the overall repression by the Germans and their French henchmen. Indeed, by 1943 the number of French workers forced to go to work in Germany had reached frightening proportions. Before the war's end, more than 750,000 had been shipped. Add to that the two million soldiers in German prison camps, and it can easily be seen that by sheer statistics, every French family had relatives or close friends in German hands. Furthermore, the "shipments to the East" of Jews were assumed to be to work camps, not to death camps. As the killing of hostages taken at random became more and more common, the hatred of the general public grew apace. Those hostages often were comprised of Jews, Communists, and anarchists, all branded as terrorists and criminals by Vichy authorities as well as the Germans, but they were also seen by many as martyrs.

If Bolsheviks and Jews died side by side before firing squads, they were also the objects of intensive official vilification, the Jews in particular. Reproductions of posters and visual propaganda materials show the Jew as hooked-nosed, snarling, and fat with rich foods and wealth. He is a war-monger who has financed war and profited greatly from it. He is the agent of destruction whose greed stops at nothing. One cartoon strip marked 1890 shows the arrival of a penniless Jew from Eastern Europe at the Gare de l'Est. He has nothing but the clothes on his back and a sack in his hand. In the second drawing, 1900, he is well dressed and sells clothing to a blonde woman on the street. By number three, 1905, he is dressed like a plutocrat and stands on the balcony of an expensive apartment, the blonde woman at his side, and a department store with *Levy* in large letters on it back of him. He has gone from rags to riches, but is still not satisfied. In 1914, munitions are his next venture. He stands, big cigar in mouth, beside artillery shells outside a factory named Levy. In 1935, he has entered politics, lecturing on peace, but behind his back consorting with thugs in the acquisition of money from war and strife. In the final episode of this *un*comic strip, dated 194?, the Jew and his money are being booted out of France.[6]

From propaganda such as this to accusations that the shortages the French population were undergoing were due to the speculations of the Jews was a short step.

Posters proclaimed that the Jews were never behind the plow, but always at the stock exchange speculating on the fruit of the farmers' labors, on wheat, wine, and vegetables. De Gaulle is depicted, face hidden by a microphone, in a poster entitled "The True Face of Free France" (*Le vrai visage de la "France Libre"*) surrounded by the usual cartoon figures of the ugly Jewish business men sneering from under their silk top hats. A series of names interspersed with Stars of David form a backdrop, and a message proclaims de Gaulle as the "quartermaster of the Jews who has cabled the rabbi Dr. Wise in New York that after the war all Israelites will be restored to their former positions and rights."[7]

It was published under the auspices of the Institut D'études des Questions Juives, which quickly began publication of rabidly anti-Semitic booklets and tracts. It also organized an exhibition in Paris of "The Jew in France." The Jews were represented as the controllers of French cinema and the puppet-masters of the Third French Republic from the year of defeat by Prussia in 1870 on, and, of course, were the scapegoats for the defeat of 1940.

Surprisingly enough, the official German propaganda magazine, *Signal*, concentrated its attacks on the Communists rather than the Jews. Published in Paris, as was the English edition, the work was obviously designed to reach a literate and presumably fairly affluent public whose fears of Bolshevism or of American economic imperialism could be exploited. The Germans were depicted as the defenders of European tradition and culture, and the central figures in the creation of a European federation that would be beneficial for all.[8]

It is interesting to compare the pre-war French magazine

Match, under German-Collaboration control during the Occupation and subsequently retitled the *Paris Match* still being published today. The formulas of both publications are surprisingly similar in structure, content, and attitudes. The *Match* of December 1938 contains a hefty portion of international politics. The front cover is of Count Galeazzo Ciano, Mussolini's son-in-law and head of foreign affairs. A lengthy article, with many photographs, documents his marriage and rise to power. In the publication, one of the first things to strike the eye is a photo of President Roosevelt carving a Thanksgiving turkey at Warm Springs, Georgia. At his side are wife Eleanor and a youthful polio victim, Robert Rosenbaum. A subtitle announces in bold print that the President is eating the traditional turkey with "a little Jew eleven years old." Before doing the carving, however, Roosevelt read a telegram from comedian Eddie Cantor telling him that he was happy to be living in a country where the object of the carving was a turkey rather than a map. The article then declares Roosevelt's delight in being able to direct an arrow at his favored *bête noire*, the Nazis. There is also a well-illustrated section on French music hall and film stars, including Claudette Colbert and Lily Pons, by then already figures familiar to American audiences. There is a long article on Tyrone Power and Loretta Young's roles in the film *Suez*. It is followed by horrifying photos of Japanese brutality and massacre in China. The back cover shows a French Legionnaire. Clearly a mixture of the increasingly serious and menacing subjects of war, actual or impending, plus the distractions of popular entertainment.

A year later, in the sixteenth week of war, still known as the "phoney war," the tone is much more somber. The

Soviet invasion of Finland has a featured place. On the lighter side is a lengthy article, with many photos, on Hollywood. Hedy Lamarr, Dietrich, Myrna Loy, Joan Bennett, Linda Darnell, and Dorothy Lamour grace the pages, accompanied by the likes of Bruce Cabot, Tyrone Power, and Leslie Howard. In a full page cartoon, a little girl asks her mother, who is trimming a Christmas tree, if Hitler has any children. In the final issues of *Match* before the fall of France, the combination of war and film dominates the pages. In one curious picture, however, there is a presentiment of things soon to come. In the issue of March 24, 1940, barely six weeks before the Nazi invasion of the Low Countries on May 10 and then of France, a glum Marshal Pétain, ambassador from France, sits silently side by side in Madrid with Herr von Stohrer, ambassador from Germany, at ceremonies celebrating the first anniversary of Pope Pius XII's coronation. Ironically enough, on June 21st it was the same Pétain who asked for an armistice with the victorious Germans.

Equally ironic are the articles on the "invincible" Maginot Line in which the French military placed so much undeserved faith, and the featured article on the fact-finding mission to Germany and France by Roosevelt's special envoy, Sumner Welles. A surprise visitor to Welles's private railway car was none other than Joseph Kennedy, then ambassador to Great Britain and short-sighted apologist for Hitler.

Once the German blitzkrieg had swept away Allied politicians' illusions, *Signal* and papers and magazines under direct or indirect German control became the official publications. Britain and America had to be transformed from Allied status to enemy, of France as well as

137

Germany. If French open collaboration could not be obtained, neutrality not requiring military intervention had to be maintained.

Signal was published in twenty languages. At its apogee in 1943, the year of decisive victories for the Allies and defeats for the Axis, it reached a readership of two and a half million. It was under the direct tutelage of the Propaganda Ministry of Goebbels in Berlin. Its English and French editions were published in Paris, where it had editorial offices until just before the capital was liberated.[9]

While the Nazis were winning victory after victory, the magazine showed scene after scene of triumphant German soldiers. In 1941, the Balkans are featured. Smiling Bosnian women hail their liberators from Serbian conspiracy and terrorism. Croatian and Moslem allies welcome German victory, while in an editorial, we are told that Germany must be the leader of a new Europe whose "liberty" must be defended by all its people! The founding of the new state of Croatia by the Oustachis is hailed with photos glorifying such details as the oath of loyalty to party and country taken on a dagger and pistol lying crossed in front of the figure of the crucified Christ.

All is not war and conflict, however. To lighten up the tone, there are articles on film, on fashion, and the tale of a kitten and a puppy. There are articles on medicine and nature. The Germans, the magazine asserts, were, after all, protective of nature, just as they were of folk and native culture, that of the Croatians, for example. The British are shown in defeat, both on land and sea.

Information on the fortifying of the Atlantic coast begins as early as a year before the D-Day invasion.

Various photographs stress the impregnability of "The Bastion of Europe." At the same time, the struggle against the Bolsheviks continues to get ample attention. The massacre of Polish officers at Katyn is shown in all its grisly horror, while for the western front, bodies of French civilians outside a Paris Metro station point an accusing finger at the crimes attributed to American Flying Fortress excesses. There is a profile of a French volunteer fighting the Russians on the eastern front. The scrapping of the luxury liner *Normandie*, rebaptized *Lafayette* before its capsizing in a major (and accidental) fire whilst being refitted in U.S. for troop carrying, provides the editors with the opportunity to attack Roosevelt and the Americans for their hostility toward France and the French empire.

Despite the magnitude of the battles fought in 1943 and such German defeats as that at Stalingrad at the end of January, *Signal* continued to show the smiling, confident, and efficient soldier, even to the point of an article on the "new European soldier," in other words, troops from various countries enlisted in the legions fighting against the Soviets. German matériel fills whole pages. There is no sign of defeat or impending disaster. War takes on an almost pastoral look, except for the coverage of the bombing of German cities. Not only is this acknowledged, it is trumpeted as terrorism, but hard-working Germans, smiling and confident despite their sufferings at the hands of a brutal enemy, clean up the destruction and courageously carry on their daily affairs. Vicissitudes cannot break the noble spirit of the generous and far-thinking German people with their astute and perceptive Nazi leaders, men of foresight shown with their families, in friendly reunions with officers and troops, and going about their exalted tasks of building a new and better Europe. Needless to say, that idyllic world existed only in *Signal*'s pages.

The reality, we know, was quite different. German medicine was busy carrying out its gruesome experiments on its hapless victims. German soldiers were massacring non-combatants. The rhythms of murder in Eastern Europe, as with the Jews, were maintained by a rigid quota system that accepted everyone as its victims, from the smallest child to the aged and infirm. Britain had suffered a blood-bath of bombings and submarine warfare that knew no quarter. While articles on films, concerts, and cultural events extolled German accomplishments in the arts, rigid controls over creativity prevailed.

Much of the truth was concealed from the general public. People refused to believe the stories of genocide, but in France as hostage killings, forced labor, and depor-tations accelerated, everybody knew the oppressiveness of the regime that pretended to be a savior of French as well as European integrity. More and more people braved the severe penalties to listen to the BBC; people saw and people talked. Meanwhile, underground presses prolifer-ated. Tracts, newspapers, and even books were published clandestinely. Vercors's fictional rendering of what was in store for France under a victorious Germany was the subject of his widely read and acclaimed short story, *The Silence of the Sea*. Even the German officer of the occupa-tion forces billeted with the French father and daughter comes to recognize Germany's intention to subjugate all of France, to be its master and to control every phase of its life once victory and mastery of the Continent were achieved.

By August 1944, as Third Army burst into Brittany and

across the plains of France toward the north and east, there were those who welcomed the Allies and those who were too deeply committed to collaborationist causes to withdraw, but to believe in German victory at such a point was either sheer blindness or simple stupidity.

Nevertheless, given such a complex political background, it is hardly surprising our military authorities worried that many of the French would be hostile because of our bombardments. They were concerned about the success of German propaganda. They need not have worried. The astonishing thing is that the French, often rightly saddened by their overwhelming losses in lives as well as property, saw the death and destruction as inevitable to their liberation and that of their country. Hopes and expectations were high. This was the heartland of the France we entered.

Notes

1. The United States of America has the honor of being the first country to grant citizenry full rights, including Jews, in 1776. France came second, and Holland was third, in 1796. Belgium granted the same rights in 1830, but England not until 1860, Austria, 1867, Germany in 1871, and the Soviet Union in 1917, also the result of Revolution.
2. Marrus-Paxton, xi.
3. Marrus-Paxton, 165.
4. Marrus-Paxton, 196–7.
5. Marrus-Paxton, 209.
6. Various pieces of visual propaganda are reproduced in *1940–1941 La France pays occupé*, a compilation of articles by various writers dealing with the Occupation in its first two years. The sections on anti-Semitism and the racial laws and their roots in pre-war France are contained in pages 673 to 695. The poster connecting de Gaulle to Jewish "backers" is on page 567.

The propaganda reproductions in the book are juxtaposed with photos of what was actually happening to the Jews of France, photos of Jews behind barbed wire enclosures, emaciated and starving, their faces filled with despair. This juxtaposition heightens the despicability of the propaganda's gross distortions.

7. The cablegram reads as follows on the poster: "Grand Rabbin Dr. Wise New York. Je prends l'engagement de réinstaller après la guerre les isréalites dans tous leurs droits et situations en France. Signed: de Gaulle.

8. The information in this section is based on the three volumes of selected materials from the English version of *Signal* listed in the bibliography, plus an almost complete set of the issue in French, which I have on a sort of extended loan from a French friend, Alexander Koltchak. Alex, who long lived and worked in the USA before returning to Paris, is the grandson of Admiral Alexander Vassilievich Koltchak, the last commander of the White Russians against the Bolsheviks. Like many another family of White Russian émigrés in France, the Koltchaks had followed the German advance into the Soviet Union as an attack against their archenemies, the Communists. The Koltchak family had purchased *Signal* regularly, but with the Liberation and the reprisals against collaborators, the family had thrown out all their copies. Alex was outraged, as he had enjoyed the magazine. Another family, no doubt glad to get the tainted materials out of their house, gave their collection to Alex. Unfortunately, there are only numbers 3 and 9 of the 1944 publication among them. As editorial headquarters had to be moved from Paris as the Allies advanced toward the capital in August 1944, number 9 may well be the final one printed in France.

The collection also contains several copies of the pre-war *Match*, and copies of an American counterpoint to *Signal* entitled *Voir* and published both in Paris and London. The issues are numbered, but not dated. One, apparently of April 1945, features Roosevelt on its cover and Truman on the facing page inside. The death of FDR had just happened, and articles proclaim the continuation of American policies. There are photos of America and of American GIs enjoying the luxuries of bath and comfortable bed in Paris.

9. S. L. Mayer is the editor of the three English volumes of selections of *Signal*. I have drawn on his introductions for information as well as on the copies of the French edition in my possession.

XIII

GOING FROM Vendôme onto the main road that runs south-west to Orleans, you pass through a town named Ouzouer-le-Marché. As the name suggests, this is a marketing center, and has been so for a long, long time. We drove straight through it in 1944, I suppose, but on returning there for the fiftieth anniversary celebrations, the local inhabitants told me about the night that General Patton had slept in a tent just on the edge of the city. Everyone is very proud of that and of having been liberated by Third Army, but there are a few skeptics. Probably not true, said several people. It's a good story anyway, said I. Our George Washington seems to have done a lot of sleeping here, there, and everywhere as well. Some true, some not, but a matter of local pride all the same.

Orleans, of course, is a real city with a fine cathedral, but we weren't on a tour, and so we drove on beyond, upriver on the Loire to the town of Gien. Perched above it is a late fifteenth-century chateau that saw a lot of French history and famous people, including Louis XIV and his mother during the revolt of the Fronde in the seventeenth century. Since the early nineteenth century, it has been known for its earthenware factory. Between 1940 and 1944, it suffered various bombardments, but otherwise was unknown to us except as a spot on the map through which we were to pass on our route to Montargis and Sens. Our stop there was brief, but it could have been history in the making, the surrender of tens of thousands of German troops to a handful of intelligence men.

As I recall it was Sunday, August 27th, just after the liberation of Paris. Any doubts we might have had about the state and condition of the Germans to the south of the Loire were eradicated there and then.

Some German officers apparently had learned that our Intelligence teams were coming through and had crossed to the north bank to make contact with us. They wanted us as representatives of Third Army to cross over with them to negotiate terms for the surrender of their units. What a moment of triumph, the Germans officers requesting that we accept their defeat and surrender! What, however, could we do with them? Where would we put them? A group as small as ours could not even conceive of such a thing. All we could do was tell them that they would have to await a larger unit and higher ranking officers to surrender. In the meantime, they were to stay south of the river until a proper surrender had been worked out. That must have taken some time, as the first noted crossing of the Loire by Americans in that vicinity downriver was well into September.

This was a pattern to be increasingly played out as Third Army moved on from one stunning victory to another. As the history books point out, however, Third Army had bypassed enemy pockets of potential serious resistance in a series of "lightning raids." German strength had been local forces rather than fully massed army units.[1] The worst was still to come.

145

At Gien, we turned north-east and left the Loire, that fluvial right flank Patton had astutely predicted would hold firm and did. Patton's luck? Perhaps, but not only thanks to the General's wisdom, of course, but with the aid of air raids on enemy troops and heroic efforts by the French FFI.[2] It did not worry us as we headed on across France in the direction of Champagne, the famous wine country, but also a region that had been a traditional invasion route for millennia, the site of battlefields and cemeteries of World War I that strike the memory and still can move to tears. We were heading to Sens, Troyes, and then on to Chalons-sur-Marne. A listing of the good-sized towns and cities liberated in this period is nothing short of extraordinary:

Orleans	16 August
Chateaudun	17 August
Pithiviers	21 August
Sens	22 August
Montargis	23 August
St. Florentin	25 August
Joigny	25 August
Troyes	26 August
Vitry-le-François	28 August
Chalons-sur-Marne	29 August
St. Dizier	31 August
Bar-le-Duc	31 August
Commercy	31 August
St. Mihiel	1 September
Joinville	2 September
Toul	5 September
Pont-à-Mousson	6 September
Nancy	15 September[3]

Every GI had heard of champagne, that bubbly liquid that constantly filled Hollywood stars' stemmed glasses, emblematic of luxury and the good life. We knew next to nothing about Champagne the region except for the city of Reims. It is safe to assume that almost every schoolchild in the USA in the 1920s and 1930s had seen pictures of the famous cathedral so badly damaged by the "Huns" in World War I. Most of us had contributed precious pennies to the reconstruction and restoration of the basilica and never expected to be near it or see it, unless we were somehow lucky enough to win a lottery. Otherwise, the cities toward which we headed were just pinpoints on a map to us, at least until we reached them. Reims, as we were soon to learn, was only one cathedral town among several on our path.

Militarily, things were still going well. The weather continued to be glorious, and Patton's "tour of France" seemed destined to go on indefinitely. Sens, seventy miles to the north-east of Orleans on the Yonne River, had been taken by famed 4th Armored on the afternoon of August 21st. At the same time, Patton was developing a plan to go straight on to Germany. The problem of supplies was growing more and more acute, however, so much so that even the general, usually uninterested in such matters, had to give serious attention to G-4's warnings.

In Sens, our teams were billeted in the Hotel de Paris et de la Poste just up the street from the cathedral. Until a few days before, the hotel had been the seat of power of the occupying forces, the German Kommandantur and Feld-gendarmerie. I had a kind of attic room which had the advantage of an impressive view of one tower of the

Gothic cathedral, St. Etienne, one of France's most beautiful, which alone would have made my short stay there memorable.

The liberation of the city had not been without its dramatics. According to one account,[4] German officers enjoying a Sunday stroll in the square in front of the Cathedral had been astonished by the "blitz" arrival of the Americans. This was capped a day later with a visit by none other than Patton himself, still piqued at not having been allowed to free Paris. The general conferred Bronze Stars on several men and went on to admire the stained glass windows of the church.[5]

French sources present a somewhat different picture of the day.[6] Sens had been occupied since June 1940, and there had been both representatives of the Vichy government and a German military administration. The results were similar to those throughout France. The full impact of the Occupation fell on the population: agricultural requisitioning that stripped farmers of their produce for shipment to Germany, rationing for the French who often found stores empty of even the official allotment, in 1943 registration of all young men for possible obligatory work service in Germany and forced participation in guarding rail lines against sabotage. After D-Day, restrictions became ever more severe. The use of electricity was drastically curtailed. Movie houses, already allowed to operate only three days a week, were to have only one showing per day. Even more stringent were the restrictions on travel by car, motorcycle or motorbike.

Sens had been bombarded by the Allies on June 23 and June 25. The target had been the important rail link between Troyes and Orleans, and the main bridge over the

Yonne River. Both were high-altitude bombings, the first of twenty-six bombs, two of which hit the targeted rail lines, and the second of twenty bombs, some of which destroyed their target, the bridge.

Unfortunately, and inevitably in such matters, bombs also hit outside the target area destroying several factories, a part of a seminary in which Germans were lodged, and some houses. Two more raids on July 8th and 16th did more damage which the Vichy authorities and the Germans did their best to utilize as anti-Allied propaganda. Collaborationist newspapers tried grimly to turn the population against their future liberators, publishing long lists of the dead and wounded, but most of the people stood firm, here as they had in Normandy, in their adherence to the Allies. Resistance groups had been organized as early as 1941 by the Communists and were joined by numbers of non-Communists. The number of Resistance fighters by summer 1944 had grown to over 5000 in the region. There had been extensive sabotage and savage repression by both the Germans and their French colleagues in the hated Milice, but that did not stop the French resistance in its efforts. Overall, Eisenhower himself estimated their power to be the equivalent of fifteen divisions, and said that the FFI's work in helping us cross France had greatly facilitated the rapidity with which we moved.[7]

Monday, August 21st, was market day in Sens, with cloudy skies that looked like rain. Everyone had been wondering how close the Americans were. That day at about noon, the radio confirmed that Third Army was about fifteen miles east of Orleans, nearing Montargis, fifty-one kilometers or twenty-three miles to the south.

The Germans were still in the city, and seemed to be doing little or nothing to defend the city or themselves against the approaching enemy forces. People were both hopeful and apprehensive.

Thanks to an eye-witness account by a non-com of the XII Corps, Corporal John Guint, we have a detailed description of Third Army's arrival in Sens:[8]

The 6th Cavalry Regiment was a reconnaissance unit that General Patton called "his eyes, his nose, his ears"; indeed, we were always one, two or three hours from the main body of Third Army forces.

After the breakthrough of German forces at St. Lô [in Normandy], we headed towards Alençon, Le Mans, and Nogent-le-Rotrou in the direction of Chartres. We waited there for 15 hours for General Leclerc's division. We then took up our advance on Orleans and Montargis before getting to Sens.

Our unit was characterized by its rapidity and mobility: it was actually composed of armed jeeps, half-tracks and M8s (an armed vehicle with 37mm cannons and heavy machine-guns). Furthermore, all of our vehicles had been tinkered with by unit mechanics to make them more rapid and more autonomous. We were accompanied by a Piper reconnaissance plane. Our combat had been primarily a pursuit racing after a German army in continuous retreat. All the same, there were often skirmishes in certain towns due to the presence of German stragglers and elements of protection for the Germans which were to hold up our advance.

Morale in the Third Army was good and General Patton very popular with his men.

The Pipers informed us that Sens was not occupied by the Germans in any force, and we went down the Chemin-Neuf to Paron [the square now named for Patton].

The populace had heard the sound of planes coming over and were relieved to find that they were the two small Piper observation planes. The French Maquis, in the meantime, was able to establish contact with one of the pilots to set up a rendezvous with members of the Resistance and Third Army units on the road coming in from Montargis.

In addition to the view of the cathedral tower every morning on awakening, I had the pleasure of meeting two good French conversationalists. One was the canon of the cathedral, Monsieur de Lagneau, a man who was a great admirer of Marie Antoinette and had a sculpted bust of her in his dining room. He was also a connoisseur of Green Chartreuse and introduced me to its pleasures. The second man was René Marin, now living with his wife and daughter in Paris, which almost prevented me finding him again. He became a close and stimulating friend, as he was half a century earlier. René and I both had an interest in international politics, a subject obviously charged with dynamite in those cataclysmic times, and we got together several evenings to talk, sip wine, and smoke numerous unfiltered American cigarettes. René, whose penchant for politics stood him well professionally in his strategic position in the Center for Economic Studies in Paris, worked with famed economist Eugene Schueller in lobbying and legislating taxing energy such as gasoline rather than value-added taxes.

Marin gives the following account of the liberation and first days of freedom in his native city:

For several days, we had been awaiting the arrival of American troops, with a certain uneasiness concerning the attitude of the German soldiers still in the city. But on the 20th of August, the latter had completely disappeared except for a handful of veterans staying in the technical college in the center of Sens, but who were readying a bus to get away.

They did not have the time to do so as the American troops arrived August 21st, and the population, having heard of it a few hours earlier, was already in the streets. The German veterans were neutralized by a Patton tank and were taken prisoner. They may have been hoping for that, since for them that represented the end of the war.

The American troops then headed on toward Troyes. The people of Sens in their relief showed their joy and acclaimed the liberating soldiers.

I don't remember exactly how we two [René and Hugh] met, but I think it was through a series of requests for information concerning the presence of the last German soldiers staying at the college. As you spoke French quite well and as I was preparing entry exams for the School of Political Science, we quickly became friends. Then you came to the house and also to my aunt and uncle's house, and I think you must have met my brother who was older than I and who was an escaped prisoner [from the Germans]. As a

152

matter of fact, it was my mother who helped him escape from the hospital in Lille where he was being held prisoner.

Your role in the Intelligence Service required you to inform yourself on the mentality of the population and also the political dynamics of Sens and particularly of the makeup of the new city administration. I recall reassuring you on this as all of the political tendencies were represented in that administration, and the mayor designate was a moderate socialist.

After that, we corresponded and when I was mobilized in turn, you tried to meet me in 1945, unsuccessfully, at the barracks at Rueil Malmaison near Paris. Given my strong interest in politics, I must admit to spending 14 hours a day at the trial of Marshal Pétain taking place in the High Court. I remember too that later on I sent a Remington razor to you in the USA because I could not get it repaired in Paris.

To finish, we were able to get in touch once more thanks to a high school friend who tried to phone me to wish me a happy birthday; that is what put me in contact with Christian Couppé. And a final coincidence: [my daughter] Isabelle is in the same class with the daughter of one of your old friends [Anne Charlotte Bougenaux].[9]

We then went on to Troyes – liberated by Combat Command A of the 4th Armored Division on August 25th, the day Paris was freed – where we made only a short stop. There had been some fierce street fighting, but little damage. Chalons-sur-Marne was my next stopping place. It was taken on the 28th. The rapid advance was continuing, but not for much longer.

The problem of supplies, and particularly of fuel, was now becoming critical. As we moved confidently towards Germany, we were also moving away from the sources of supply in the Normandy region. This was crucial. An army that depended on gasoline could not go ahead without it. Ironically enough, in a matter of a few days, Third Army had overrun the very areas where German armies had been brought to a standstill in World War I. In that conflict, hundreds of thousands of men perished trying to gain only a few yards of ground; now we rolled over with "lightning" speed near the ground where the trenches stayed in place for almost four long and bloody years. In 1944, however, those of us with Patton not only swept through the area; we were ready to go straight on to the Siegfried Line fortifications, certain that we could penetrate the final defenses of German soil with low casualties.

Sadly enough for everyone except the Germans, Patton was to be thwarted in what became a bitter struggle with SHAEF over who was to get and to do what. As summer ended, so did Third Army's blitzkreig. Advances were to become more costly, weather and terrain hindering operations already crippled by the shortages of gas and ammunition.

I was not the only one to remember the weather, the boredom, and the creeping fears. Writing about Nancy, and reflecting what was to become our standard experience from this time on, the XII Corps history recounts:

The only really unpleasant elements [in Nancy], aside

from the German railway gun, about which more anon, were the waiting, the worry and the weather. The waiting and worry, after the relatively carefree race across France, bore heavily on the HQ but not much could be done about them. And nothing, of course, could be done about the weather. This last was lousy; incredible amounts of rain and constant raw cold. After the middle of the month, grey overcast days began; "it was winter from then on." Everyone who could moved in under cover.[10]

Any kind of protection from the cold and rain, even in buildings without any windows left, was preferable to being out in a tent. The mud was all-pervasive:

Col. Scanlon carried away vivid recollections of Nancy: "The weather was most horrible. Men came in covered in mud from head to foot. The day after we came into Nancy, Lt Rigg's driver, Jerry Capone, was killed when his jeep rolled over a mine. This was our first KIA."[11]

My own experience, aside from walking and wading in mud in the country villages where we checked out the situation on a daily basis, was that of stepping into what appeared to be a shallow ditch of water. I immediately sank almost to hip level in mud and had to be pulled out, filthy dirty.

Despite such hindrances, however, Patton still managed some incredible feats. Two rivers that had become part of World War I lore, the Marne–Chalons, Reims, and Troyes were behind it by August 29 – and the Meuse that traverses Verdun. Two even more crucial rivers to be taken and held lay on ahead, the Moselle and the Meurthe, before getting to the Rhine. Patton was fully aware of the importance of those rivers, as were the Germans opposing us.

Chalons-sur-Marne was liberated one week after Sens on Monday, August 28th, eighty-three days after the invasion. A large cache of cognac had also been liberated, and as was fairly typical of Patton, orders were given to distribute quantities of it to all of us. With our generous portion of Norman Calvados long gone, this was more than welcome as the weather grew cold and raw and the resistance to our advance strengthened.

Chalons stands in the very heart of the Champagne region and, like its neighbors, is noted for wine, for its churches, art, and the canals that make it another miniature Venice. It suffered in both world wars, but still retains treasures worth seeing. The hotel where our teams were billeted has since been replaced by a bank building, but around the corner from it is the house where Marie Claude Grenier lived. I had met Marie Claude on a Sunday morning in the bar of the little hotel to get a cup of morning coffee, such as it was in those days. There was an employee at the bar and two women and a man sitting at a table. Otherwise, no one. I was not unduly surprised when one of the young women walked over and in halting English invited me to join her sister and brother-in-law at their table. Once seated, I listened as Marie Claude struggled with her English, and finally I relented and explained that I spoke French. A friendship began.

Marie Claude invited me and any fellow GIs who wished to come with me to her home for a party that afternoon. Where all of the others had gone that Sunday was and is a mystery to me, but the only buddy around was Ralph Palmer of CIC who was to be, and is, a close friend. There were almost no men at the party except the two of us, and so we basked in the admiration of a bevy of girls all excited at getting to know a couple of American soldiers. We were invited to come back after our evening meal.

That night, Marie Claude's mother played the piano and we all sang such songs popular at the time as *J'ai ta main dans ma main*, until the father came home and pointed out that we had not been given good enough champagne. He proceeded to take us into his extensive cellar – he was a wine merchant – and to pick out the very best for Chalons' liberators. It was an evening not to be forgotten.

I saw more of Marie Claude before going on to Toul. The house where she lived still stands on the Rue Grenier à Sel, but its occupants are no longer the Grenier family. The present owner showed me through the downstairs, even to the little alcove where the piano stood and the door to the cellars where the wines and champagne had been kept. Marie Claude married a general, and died several years ago.

Toul is another cathedral town not far to the west of Nancy. For most GIs of Third Army, it is justly remembered for a concert that Bing Crosby performed there in a big warehouse. When he ended the show with *White Christmas*, "there wasn't a dry eye in the place," CIC buddy Ralph Palmer recalls.

Our taking of Toul was important because of its position on the Moselle River, but its proximity to the major urban center of Nancy, fourteen miles beyond, was even more so. By this time gasoline supplies were critically low. Use of vehicles had to be kept at a minimum, but for those of us responsible for security and the gathering of information, duties that required us to be out in our jeeps in town and in country, there was limited fuel. And, despite shortages that would have crippled any other commander, Patton saw to it that the drive to take and secure the Moselle River went on, although we were running into increasingly stiff enemy resistance, to further complicate our forward drive. The river itself represents a formidable obstacle, growing wider and swifter as it heads north towards its fusion with the Rhine.

The 80th Infantry had forced its way across the river at Pont-à-Mousson, half-way between Nancy and the stronghold city of Metz to the north, but lacking artillery or armored reinforcements because of the shortages, an enemy counterattack resulted in a heavy and bloody loss of men. Nevertheless, by September 7th, small bridgeheads to the north and south of Toul had been secured, but the supply problem made further progress here, and elsewhere, impossible. Where progress was made, it was at a very heavy cost.[12]

We actually entered Nancy on September 14th, but only after fierce fighting on the outskirts, but the 15th is given as the official liberation date. Sniper fire continued to be a problem for days afterwards, and a long-range railway cannon fired into the city, causing considerable damage. Some accounts say it was destroyed by artillery on October 21st. Photos, however, show buildings in Nancy severely damaged on October 24, and the shelling of Morhange, or Mörchingen as the Germans named the town, further on,

158

took place well into December.[13] The gun was even given a name:

> Like the famous "Paris Gun" of World War I, the "Nancy Gun" of World War II was largely a harassing agent. It produced relatively few casualties for the effort expended, but it certainly cost XII Corps headquarters and closely associated units a lot of lost sleep. The thing was a 280mm Railway gun, located somewhere to the northeast of Metz in the XX Corps zone, and it lobbed those big noisy shells 'way down into Nancy, landing them all around the CP area.[14]

Two days earlier, eighty-nine German planes had flown over Nancy, but dropped no bombs.[15] Fighting continued, increasing in intensity, within a few miles of the city, and agents were parachuted behind our lines, including an Alsatian who was easily persuaded to act as a double agent.

It was not until November 7th when the battle for Germany and the Rhineland began that Third Army was given its head once again. In the meantime, much valuable time had been lost. The Germans had had time to reorganize and to reinstall the Siegfried Line to the north of the German border. Patton asserted, undoubtedly quite correctly, that if Third Army had been furnished with adequate supplies, the advance towards the Frankfurt-Mainz-Darmstadt region would have made the German counteroffensive in the Ardennes an impossibility. That, however, was not how history played it.

Notes

1. Farago. *Patton*, in chapter 29.
2. Colonel Allen, in his *Lucky Forward*, describes General Manton S. Eddy's concerns with this matter when he took over command of Third Corps, and Patton's reply to his question about this: "Manton," he said, "if I had worried about flanks, we'd all still be sitting in the hedgerows in Normandy. You have an open flank, but it's nothing to worry about. First of all, the enemy is on the run. Second, he has nothing south of you mobile enough to make an attack in strength before our air can spot it. [G-2 estimated German strength south of the Loire as equivalent to three Infantry divisions with 22,000 combat effectives.] The thing for you to do is to advance in depth, one division echeloned behind the other. That will give you striking power and at the same time cover your flank." (p. 117)
3. Dyer, 188. The date of the liberation of Sens given in French sources is the 28th, as I say below.
4. Farago, 561.
5. Farago, 560–1.
6. Detailed information comes from a booklet published by the College Mallarmé of Sens, *Le siège de Sens en 1814* and *La libération de Sens (21 août 1994)* by Travaux Pédagogiques 1984. It was given to me by my friend from Sens of half a century, René Marin, of whom I write below.
7. Dyer, 188, 192.
8. Reproduced in French, which I translate, in the Sens *Libération* book 59–60. What little information on Guint himself the article gives implies that he came back to live in Sens, probably as in most cases, by marrying a local girl. I reproduce the information as given, but have not been able to verify what Guint writes about being part of the "6 regiment de cavalerie," which is characterized as a reconnaissance unit.
9. René Marin, letter dated Paris, July 14, 1993. Marin authored a book entitled *Application de l'impôt sur l'énergie, Elements chiffres*, Préface de Eugène Schueller, published in Paris by the Centre d'Etudes Economiques, 1953.

160

10. Dyer, 232, 234.
11. Dyer, 234.
12. *Lucky Forward* says that the numbers of wounded and dying in hospitals was so great at this period that a special convoy had to be sent back to the Normandy beach area to get mattress covers in which to bury the dead, and personal effects bags for their belongings.
13. Dyer, *XII Corps*, 95.
14. Dyer, *XII Corps*, 240.
15. In Province, 71 and 74.

XIV

A S WE WAITED in Toul to go on to Nancy, we were billeted, as in Vendôme, in what had been the German Soldatenheim. In this case, however, the building was not a hotel but a mansion that contained some impressive tapestries and furniture. It was the type of residence that once must have belonged to a well-to-do cultured Jewish family. No owners ever showed up to claim their home, either then or later. A dentist now occupies the premises. From the families we got to know, we heard the by now commonplace stories of parachutists and hidings, of radioing information out to us as we approached, and so on.[1]

Nancy was the biggest city in France I had been in. We were billeted in the old Hotel Theirs, now torn down, across from the railway station. Somewhere along the way, probably in the barracks where the Germans had been stationed in Bar-Le-Duc, I had "liberated" a portable phonograph and some records, one of *Septembre sous la Pluie* by singer Léo Marjane whom I was to meet years later in New York. The music was a solace on lonely evenings alone, when the dark made the strange city, all blacked out of course, seem ominous compared to the smaller towns we had been in.

Our G-2 offices were in the Hotel de Ville (City Hall),

on the Place Stanislas, rightly reputed one of Europe's most beautiful squares. It is one that reflects to a degree Lorraine's checkered and often turbulent history. The northern half of the region epitomizes that history. It had a German name, Lotharingen. Even today, in Morhange, for example, photo shops display postcards of the Kaiser's visit to the city before World War I, then as during the 1940s incorporated into Germany from 1871 to 1918. It had been incorporated again into Germany, along with all of Alsace, from June 1940 until the Liberation of 1944. French-speaking natives were forcibly evacuated to other parts of France and forbidden to return to their homes, which were confiscated with their belongings. Only German was to be spoken, publicly or privately. All education, films, meetings, and the like were conducted in German. The swastika became as ubiquitous as in the Reich.

Severe penalties were imposed for all infractions. Among other crimes that resulted in deportation to work camps in Germany were speaking French in public, wearing a beret, helping a prisoner of war, or insulting the Nazi party. And although Nancy was south of the line of the territory of Lorraine that was annexed, it too was in Nazi plans for integration into Hitler's Thousand Year Reich. With good reason: the region of which it is the center is rich in heavy industry as well as agriculture, and iron, coal, and salt.

By European standards, Nancy is not a particularly ancient city. It was founded by the dukes of Lorraine in the eleventh century, and in the fourteenth century passed into the hands of the dukes of Burgundy. There were battles and sieges. The so-called Cross of Lorraine, or Cross of Jerusalem with its double horizontal bar, became the city's emblem during one of these struggles for possession of the city, and was to become, as we know, the emblem of General de Gaulle's Free French.

By the sixteenth century, Nancy had become a religious center, but it suffered dearly in the Thirty Years War, not to recover its prestige till the seventeenth and eighteenth centuries. A curious footnote to history is the story of King Stanislas of Poland whose kingdom was divided among Prussia, Austria, and Russia, by Frederick the Great, Maria Teresa, and Catherine the Great, respectively. The monarch without a country had married his daughter to none other than Louis XV of France who proved to be a very supportive son-in-law. After the then duke of Lorraine exchanged the duchy for one in Tuscany, King Louis turned it over to his father-in-law. At Stanislas's death, the territory was to be returned to the authority of the French kingdom. And so it came to pass, but before it did, good King Stanislas endeared himself to his subjects by giving them a major heritage, among many others, of the magnificent square that bears his name. He was also a likeable man, easy-going and indulgent in matters of politics and religion, a lover of good food, good drink, and beautiful women, the embodiment of a ruler of the Age of Enlightenment.

The nineteenth and early twentieth centuries saw marked population growth for Nancy, as well as in wealth and industry. World War I brought bombardments by both planes and long-distance cannons, while the northern part of Lorraine was one of the major battlefields of that conflict, with Verdun at its core. World War II saw it as a center for troop movements, both coming and going. September 15th at 11 a.m. is given as the official date and

164

time of its liberation by Third Army. That day, Lucky Forward Headquarters moved to bivouac near Verdun. The next move for Patton and his headquarters was to Nancy. That was on October 11th, but XII Corps Headquarters had preceded it. Patton settled in in Nancy at a modest but attractive house at Number 10, Rue Auxonne, not too far from the Place Stanislas and a block distant from a major boulevard now bearing his name. Nearby on the square still stands the eighteenth-century Grand Hotel where Patton met with Eisenhower and Bradley, and which currently is rated by Michelin as Nancy's finest hostelry.

In many ways this period in the Nancy-Metz area was Third Army's low point, except for the early stages of December's Battle of the Bulge. The struggle between British Field Marshal Montgomery and Patton for supplies and authorization to take the offensive was sadly enough unsuccessful for the latter. The British commander won out over the strenuous and highly pungent objections of the American general.

Fuel and supplies as well as men and equipment were diverted to Montgomery. The weather grew increasingly inclement. The fall rains began, the climate became raw and the cold penetrating. There was mud everywhere. The roads were as slippery as sheets of ice because of it. Vehicles of all shapes and sizes were wrecked or slid off the roadways. Our offensives were brought to a halt, and with that, the Germans had time to regroup, to catch their breath, and to counterattack. Enemy agents were infiltrating our lines; great numbers of refugees of all kinds and nationalities, many on enforced labor, added to the already enormous complications of both military and civilian logistics. Our responsibilities in the area of security increased accordingly.

Meanwhile, along with the bloody battle and the losses at Pont-à-Mousson, the great fortress of the key city of Metz was under siege. It was to go on, in varying degrees of intensity, from early September until the 22nd of November. It was a major victory for XX Corps, Third Army, but at a terrible cost. The last great barrier before the Siegfried Line had fallen. The Americans had overcome the enemy despite the worst flooding in two decades, rain and poor visibility which paralyzed air operations. The fortress of Metz was captured for the first time since AD 451 when the Huns had taken it.

Our offices in Nancy in the Hotel de Ville on the Place Stanislas had the advantage of being the spot where de Gaulle spoke. The square was mobbed with cheering people, but our units had their own ringside seats inside. We were told by Resistance leaders that an equally enthusiastic crowd several weeks before had welcomed Marshal Pétain on the very spot.

A day or so after our arrival and installation, French Resistance men came to the office to turn in the radios they used for the transmission of information to us about German troops movements and military activities. That mission was not only very important, it was very dangerous not only for the men carrying it out. Had they been discovered, not only they would have been sent off to a concentration camp in Germany, their wives and children would have shared their fate. Understandably, everyone was elated to have this risky business over and the sword removed from over their head.

The central figure in this underground operation was

Hubert Payon. He felt that this second liberation from fear and danger merited a celebration, and so, accordingly, with his wife Mimi he gave a dinner party for three of us, Roland Breton, Earl Coon and myself, and for the men who had so valiantly worked with him in getting information out to us. It was a memorable evening that must have strained the Payons' budget and enriched the local black market, for we feasted beautifully and quaffed good wines and liqueurs into the wee hours. Whether our French friends could sleep it off the next morning or not I don't remember, but we had to be on duty by eight o'clock, fully accoutered as men of Patton's Third in shirt, tie, and jacket.

Over lunch in Nancy in 1993, Hubert, Mimi, and I reminisced about that night. Their son Franco was a small baby then, now a father of his own. It was the last time Payon had any further contact with the Resistance men with whom he had shared danger. The mission accomplished, each man went his own way.

One question I did not think to ask was how many of those six or eight men Hubert himself knew. Perhaps only one, for protection utmost secrecy was a very serious matter for everyone, and common practice was to restrict contact to one or two persons within a cell so that in case of arrest, what one did not know, one could not tell. Torture was routine in the Gestapo, but if the person arrested knew very little except his own operation, he could tell very little. It was not unusual for members of the same family to be working in the underground without being aware of the participation of a father, mother, sister or brother until the Liberation and freedom from pressure and fear. The stories of those who died under torture without revealing a single contact is great tribute to the courage and determination of numerous men, women, and even youngsters.

Note

1. I had remembered two families that had invited me to dinner, one Dr. Rhotan, and the other Dr. Grégoire. The latter's son lives in his parents' home across from the cathedral. Michel Hachet of the municipal museum, which has a very interesting section on both world wars and photos of the extensive destruction of the city in 1940, had known the Rhotans and Grégoires. I had recalled the Rhotans as living right beside the cathedral. That was an optical illusion, as standing in front of the house, one has the impression of having the façade of the church to the left whereas actually it is across the square from the row of houses.

XV

THE DAY after the liberation of Nancy, September 16th, as the 35th Infantry Division cleaned up pockets of enemy resistance, 137th Infantry advanced to the south-east to the small cities of St. Nicholas-du-Port, Varangéville, and Dombasle, and then on to the small city of Lunéville, site of King Stanislas's favorite chateau and twenty-one miles from Nancy. Lunéville was also liberated, but the Germans soon returned to the town and several days of battles ensued, as they did more or less around Nancy and throughout the region until into October.

This was to be home ground for some weeks as Third Army had been put on the "defensive," and ordered to come to a halt. As a consequence, the offensive against Hitler's West Wall that Patton expected to get under way on the 18th was forestalled. Meanwhile, the Germans infiltrated Lunéville and undertook a major counter-attack. General Eddy's push towards Germany became stalled, and in the short interim before his forces could regroup to begin their offensive, Montgomery won out at SHAEF. He got his way, and he got the supplies Patton wanted for us.

To the bitterness of the weather and the terrain was added the bitter defeat by politics of a plan that most of us, then and now, feel would have greatly shortened the war. The standoff, however, only increased the necessity for rigid control of the areas to which we of Intelligence were assigned. We had to know who was going where and why.

The area for which Ralph Palmer of CIC and I were made responsible was about the size of a small American county. At first we were civil government as well as intelligence. We were low in rank within the army, but we did represent Third Army and thereby the United States. This gave us authority and stature, and made us central figures in the goings-on of the area consisting, as I have mentioned, of St. Nicholas-du-Port, Varengéville, Dombasle, and the surrounding countryside.

It was to Dombasle that we headed our jeep that September morning in 1944. It was sunny. As there was so little sun that September and October, it was something to remember.

If the towers of the basilica in nearby St. Nicholas are imposing, the entry to Dombasle is in many ways even more memorable. At the approaches to the city stands an enormous factory belonging to the Belgian-owned Solvay company, manufacturers of various chemical products, and here of sodium carbonate. Separating it from the road is a port of the Meuse-Rhine Canal connecting the Meuse and Rhine Rivers filled with barges.

Founded in 1873, the Solvay plant transformed what had been a modest farming village into an industrial center, and from then on, it was Solvay around which the life of the town revolved. The company continues to dominate the town's life today, although in Dombasle as everywhere else in the industrial countries of the West, the "paternalism" of half a century ago has been considerably modified. The rows of workers' houses, for example, are privately owned now, and are considerably brighter in color and aspect than at war's end, but it is, as it was in 1944, a "company town." The company buildings are open to community use, the company hospital still stands where it did but is under a medical group's control, and the stately houses of the executives line the same street near the same railway station. The only noticeably new building is the Hotel de Ville, inaugurated by General de Gaulle in 1961. The anniversary of the Liberation has had several notable re-enactments, and surviving members of a very active Resistance group, the Groupe Lorraine 42 which operated in Nancy as well as the Dombasle area, are highly honored and respected by young and old alike.[1]

The countryside surrounding Dombasle consists of gentle rolling hills dotted with farming villages and wooded areas, hiding places for the Resistance during the Occupation, but equally available for Germans or agents if any crossed into our lines.

Life in a jeep became a daily routine as we went from town to village, and from village to farm hamlet. It was raw and cold, and often raining, but Ralph and I had the advantage of a canvas cover over our heads in the jeep, and a warm home and hot food to come back to. We had no reason to complain. In the evenings we usually were free and could go out or accept invitations. We stayed in Dombasle for some three or four weeks, a very long time for anyone to stay put in Patton's army!

To the north, we heard reports that the fighting for Metz had intensified, but we stayed in place. The order restraining Third Army, received September 25th, was to last until the 7th of November. It was a severe setback to Patton and a strategic blunder. Palmer and I knew perfectly well that the Germans had first retreated, then later returned to positions they had abandoned. Meanwhile, the town itself, except for a V-bomb that landed nearby early one morning with an earthshaking explosion, settled into an apprehensive but tranquil kind of peace.

In the time spent there, the responsibility for the security of Dombasle and the surrounding area, was, as I have said, assigned to CIC Ralph Palmer and me. When we got into the town, we went, as we had been instructed, to the mayor's office in the Hotel de Ville to see about billeting. We went in turn to the Red Cross where a gray-haired lady with glasses said that she had two bedrooms to show us. We trotted along with her to her row house at 33 Rue Solvay. A modest home, but as clean as a pin and carefully kept. In the dining room, to my surprise I spotted a photo of Hubert Payon. I exclaimed that that was a picture of my friend from Nancy. "That," said Madame Payon, which I then realized was the lady's name, "is our son. You must stay here." And so we did until Third Army once again was advancing.

As Ralph and I began daily sorties in our jeep into the hamlets and farms to guard against any infiltration by German agents and to gather information about the doings of the Germans, we learned that the enemy withdrawal had been complete. For the most part, they had departed in vehicles pulled by requisitioned horses. The prize plum of entering Germany proper, as Patton so vehemently and correctly asserted, had been temporarily ready for easy picking. All we had to do was move forward. But there was no gas, no supplies to move on.

172

Enough fuel was doled out to us to make our rounds, but we were, after all, only one jeep. In terms of advancing and of victory, the bitterness of the weather was matched by the bitterness of seeing an extraordinary opportunity slip by.

Once the Germans assessed the situation, they regrouped and refortified the Siegfried Line. The opportunity was lost. Had we advanced, however, even the Battle of the Bulge might have been thwarted at the outset. German preparations for the Ardennes offensive could get under way unimpeded. Intelligence knew, to a limited degree, about the movements that were to culminate in that fulminating attack, but did not heed the warning signs until it came on December 16th.

The Payons of Dombasle were a wonderful couple. Henri, the husband, was a male nurse in the Solvay Hospital a block and a half away from their home. Madame Payon took our C- or K-rations on her bicycle to the country where she exchanged canned goods for fresh foods. On many a raw cold night after a day in the open jeep, the hot steaming potages were more than welcome. So was the *eau-de-vie* that the farmers pressed on us in our rounds of the countryside. I acquired a taste for Mirabelle, either in liquid form or in the typical tart of the region, and for Quetch and Framboise. Strong drink for young stomachs, and very warming. One farmer's comely daughter began to make a point of serving a tot to Ralph herself while the father chatted with me, so we knew we had one stop to make each time we were in that vicinity. I recall nothing of note coming out of those visits, except for a growing appreciation of the local *eaux-de-vies*, but they are a memory to chuckle over.

On the evenings that were not overly inclement, there were street dances up in the section of workers' houses. Usually there were one or two local accordion players. I dated a dark-haired girl named Giselle, whose house still stands where it was, but who moved away many years ago. We went to a local hall where quite a few GIs had been invited to a dance. The musicians there were accordionists also. The fun piece of the evening was called "La danse du tapis," or Dance of the Rug, a kind of musical chairs in which a small rug was used by the person stuck in the middle of the dancers to choose his new partner and to return to dancing him or herself.

One family, the Audoyers, began to invite me to dinner. Bob was a vice-president of Solvay and lived in one of the company executive mansions. Bob and Bobette had no children of their own and so were particularly welcoming. When Bob's sister Maryse arrived after a harrowing trip by truck from Paris, our evenings together became even more frequent. There was an imposing hierarchy within the society of the town, primarily based on one's position in the Solvay structure. The Audoyers, in that sense, were the aristocrats, and although they themselves were totally relaxed in their social outlook, other townsfolk were aware of the differences in status. Bobette's goodbye dinner for me the night before Palmer and I left for points east is a case in point. As I tried to cut my food, the plate wobbled again and again. Trying to be polite, I said nothing for quite a while, only to learn finally that there was a little rubber air-bulb under the plate. When Police Inspector Emile Gallien came to join us for dessert, Bobette played the same trick on him. He gave no sign of his embarrassment, however, until the hostess laughingly explained what she had been doing.

Mimi, as Emile was nicknamed, was more or less our age. He and another young police officer became friendly colleagues. We relied heavily on them for enforcement of our regulations against movement between towns except with express permission. We also counted on them to help round up any person or persons crossing from the no man's land area to the north and east of us. Mimi and I became good friends, and until his recent death could still laugh about the nights we spent in the rain and darkness, arms at the ready because we had been informed that there had been infiltration by Germans in civilian clothes into Dombasle. It was real cloak-and-dagger stuff, but we ended up with nothing and no one, and had to come to the lame conclusion that our informer had bilked us on that occasion.

There were some cases we worked on that were unresolved. One was the man who crossed the lines into a neighboring village and who was brought to us for interrogation. We questioned him well into the night, making him stand, despite what we knew was a very sore heel. He told a very strange tale about his wandering through the lines. Indeed, his story made little sense, unless we saw him as some kind of poor fool unaware of the potential violence surrounding us all. Next morning, we took him to a detention-interrogation center. We heard that later he had been released as harmless, a witless fool, as we suspected.

In some of the other towns we had been in, he might well have ended up with a bullet put through him by itchy members of the Resistance, who in most cases, were far less tolerant than we Americans. Some of the *épurations* or purges became vengeful. One mayor of a small city asked me what to do with the women who had had German lovers. Some of the FFI felt that they were traitors and should be shot. I suggested that the women have their heads shaved, as had been done in quite a few towns we had passed through.

Such treatment was surely better than a bullet, but even it, as we later learned, was a cruel spectacle that sometimes ended up with physical brutality and even gang rape. Hatred of the Germans and those who collaborated with them ran high. It was understandable after the savagery of German troops, the Gestapo, and particularly the Waffen SS in their fury as they retreated. Justice was often served, but sometimes not. We often had to make decisions or give serious advice affecting many lives on little evidence and within a very short period of time. People who came from out of town were suspect for several reasons, one of them being the probability that the person was a collaborator escaping the wrath of the citizens of their previous residence.

In Dombasle, we encountered a case in point. A singularly attractive young brunette whose name was Raymonde appeared in town, as we learned from the police. Where she had come from was not well established. She had no travel permission, papers, or perceivable means of support. The story she told seemed implausible, and we wondered who she really was. Not until after we had left Dombasle did we learn the truth. She had been the mistress of a Gestapo Colonel; she had fled the town where she had lived, her clothes and furs had been publicly burned, and she had come to Dombasle where no one knew her to try to escape the wrath of the Resistance groups. She ended

176

up, Police Inspector Gallien was to tell me later, as a small-time prostitute in Nancy.

One welcome visitor in Dombasle was the Payons' second son, André, who was a priest with three parishes in villages to the south of Tours. He appeared one day in Dombasle after thirteen days on a bicycle to cross France. He had had no word about the well-being of his parents or of his brother and family. He celebrated his homecoming by making the first flaming dessert omelette I had ever seen, but he also had a terrible and somber story to tell about what had happened in one of the villages that comprised his parish. It was about the hamlet of Maillé.

The atrocity of Oradour-sur-Glane when the SS herded 642 inhabitants into the church and burned them alive is justly remembered. That had happened on June 10th, 1944. The massacre of Maillé is almost as savage. It took place on August 25th when the defeat of Germany loomed large on the horizon. Abbé Payon wrote a book published in 1945 about the event, but, of course, told us about it in all the ferocity of detail there in his parents' house in Dombasle.[2]

Notes

1. On April 21st, 1993, Christian Couppé and I drove from Lunéville, where we had spent the night, to Dombasle to the Hotel de Ville. As I tell later on in more detail, the mayor, a professor of history named Robert Blaise, had arranged through his assistant, a professor of mathematics, Claude Wrobel, for me to meet and spend the day with four highly decorated men of Groupe Lorraine 42. We were both impressed with their dignity and their pride in their activities in the underground, which they recalled with surprising clarity. Pierre Ballé, severely wounded in 1940 and again during

resistance activities at the time of the Liberation in 1944, was mayor of Dombasle from 1947 to 1959. The other men were Jean Césard, Raymond Grimm, and René Fresse. None of them remembered me nor I them from 1944, but they all knew the Payons (a street has now been named in honor of Henri Payon, the same street where Giselle Isoard lived, and we danced to the music of the accordionists) and the Audoyers. We drove to various sites in the city and countryside, the cache for arms where a monument is going up, and markers of numerous places where members of the Resistance were shot down, one with the photographs of four men shot and thrown into the nearby river.

That afternoon, there was a ceremony to welcome me given by the mayor. I was awarded a medal and was interviewed by town historian-writers Gerard Berge and Michel Caps.

2. Abbé André Payon, Curé de La Celle-Saint-Avant, Drache et Maillé. *Maillé martyr*. Tours: Arrault et Cie., 1945.

XVI

THE DETAILS that the youthful abbot recounted were horrifying and remain etched in my memory. Young André had been priest to the parishes for only about a month when the massacre took place. The village, or *bourg* of Maillé as he calls it, is in Touraine, that rich region of farmlands and vineyards and ancient stone churches that is called "the garden of France." It lies slightly to the south of the major chateau area, and of Blois and Vendôme, but shares the same mild climate and bucolic landscape. Maillé itself in 1944 was comprised of sixty buildings, with a population of 241 inhabitants made up, for the most part, of farmers. Eighty-eight refugees had come to swell that number, including thirty-four young people dodging the draft for work in Germany and who, Abbé Payon tells, had sufficient knowledge of wartime ways to restore electric current in time to listen to the forbidden broadcast of the BBC from London.

A small stream, the Reveillon, passes through the town which was crowned by the steeple of a twelfth-century romanesque church. It was the epitome of a peaceful and tranquil existence.

Just before the massacre, there had been underground activities by the Maquis in the immediate region. The nearby railway tracks had been blown up three times, and on August 11th the pilot of an English plane shot down by a railway gun had parachuted to earth and had escaped capture by German patrols complete with police dogs. Someone in that area had had to hide them, care for them, and help them to escape. Maillé was marked for reprisals, whether the "guilty" party was there or not.

On the 24th, a truckload of FFI had an encounter with two cars full of German officers. An ensuing fusillade lasted for three quarters of an hour. The inhabitants of a neighboring farm saw traces of blood on the grass, but knew nothing more about the outcome or whether the blood was French or German. All the French prefect of the *départemente* of Indre-et-Loire was told by the Feldkommandant was that there had been an attack in Maillé that had resulted in dead and wounded. The stage was set for savage reprisals.

The Feldkommandant got in touch with the Waffen SS in Tours, requesting immediate reinforcements and two 88mm cannons. The reason given for the request, and the single word that worked magic, was: "terrorists." By the following morning, everything necessary had arrived. Maillé was sealed off, and the beginnings of the massacre were postponed only because of an attack that morning by English aircraft which crippled one of the cannons and machine-gunned a locomotive. The ensuing barrage of bullets, heard clearly in the neighboring town of Sainte-Maure, was interpreted as explosions from a munitions train erroneously thought hit by the strafing.

By 10:30 a.m., however, the flames rising from Maillé made it clear that something unusual was happening in the village. The butchery had begun.

It was without mercy for age, infirmity or family. The tiny number who survived, mostly by quirk and accident, gave a grisly account of the merciless shootings, bayoneting, and throat-cutting of babies in their mothers' arms, paralyzed elderly women and men, children by the side of their dying parents, and then the village being set afire with the bodies lying unburied and untouched except by the flames. Once the butchery finally came to an end in the afternoon, the shelling by the second cannon began, until only the shells of houses and barns were left. Livestock fared no better than the martyred human beings.

Abbé Payon was particularly touched by the killing of the family he knew best, the Confolents. The father, a veteran of World War I and of 1940, survived. In the Abbé's own words:

In the center of the town across from the church, a small middle-class dwelling houses 12 persons. It is the abode of Monsieur Roger Confolent. An officer in 1914 and 1940, the recipient of five citations, twice wounded, he has the decoration of the Legion of Honor. He lives with his wife, his mother-in-law Madame Gambier, aged 84, and his seven children: Pierre, aged 22; Jéhanne, 20; Yves, 19, René, 17; Hélène, 14; Jean, 12; Claude, 11; two housemaids: Valentine Garnier, 32, and Georgette, his sister. Between the members of these young people, the happiest of harmony filled the house with charm. Myself, as priest, was cordially welcomed there. Jean and Claude were two of my choir members. Hélène played the harmonium. Jéhanne took charge of catechism.

181

But I will cede the word to Monsieur Confolent:

"By a fatal coincidence that morning we were all together. At the sound of the first gunshots, I made everyone come inside. I myself am in the kitchen with my wife, Yves, René, Hélène, and the two maids. Jéhanne with her two younger brothers, Jean and Claude, went down into the cellar where they were sheltered. The eldest boy, Pierre, was absent, no doubt hiding in a neighboring building where he was doing some work.

"Suddenly at about 11 o'clock, René, who has a very good sense of hearing and heard steps, said to me: 'Papa, here come the Germans.' And indeed we heard the door of the courtyard open. I answer, as I get to my feet: 'Fine, I'll go see. Don't move.'

"I didn't have time to get outside when a soldier, like a crazy man, burst into the courtyard and fired a machine-gun burst at me. Untouched and thinking it was a mistake, I walked towards him with my arms in the air and cried out: 'Civil, Kamarad, civil!' [civilian] when the brute took aim again, and shots rang out. Just in time to miss being hit, I threw myself over backwards. Alas, Yves rushed to my side, thinking he'd be more fortunate: 'Papa, you didn't yell loud enough. He didn't understand': arms high he yelled with all his might: 'Hier Civil, Kamarad, Civil, Civil!!!' But a burst, two bursts of gunshots are his answer, and he crumples to the ground.

"The murderer is now in the kitchen. He fires in every direction, mortally wounding René with an explosive in the right side, and Hélène in the thigh. On my advice, everyone falls to the floor and pretends to be dead. The German goes out. René's voice rises as he recites the Act of Contrition. We all join him in prayer."

The father had hoped that his wife would be spared, and some of the children, but no one survived. The Germans returned, even throwing an incendiary grenade onto the bed of the dying grandmother. Outside, he heard Madame Martin beg for the life of her infant, then shots, and silence. In the meantime the soldiers had gone into the kitchen to eat and to drink, getting some refreshmeant before going on with their carnage. Another whole family was found huddled around their mother, teenagers, small children and a baby of three months, so badly burned in what was left of their barn that the bodies could not be separated.

This was the story that young Payon brought to us that somber October, but one story stood out, with that of the Confolent family, that of a tiny baby girl. The abbot was the first person permitted by German authorities to enter the ruined village:

I was the first person they [the survivors] had seen since the massacre. I retraced my steps to see if I recognized the dead at the crossroads. Sontag's clothes were still burning. I also saw the body of Achille Barre that was no longer afire. I recognized no one else except Monsieur Millary, whose face was familiar to me. It's true I had only been in the area for a month by then. I went off to the blacksmith stall of Monsieur Martin. The savage way in which the little baby Danielle was killed made a deep impression on me. The killer must have placed the barrel of the gun under the child's neck. The little one was smiling, with arms joyfully open. The German had emptied her skull with his gunfire. The tiny body, blue eyes wide open, seemed still alive, but the whole cranium had been blown to pieces. You could only see it only when you turned over the cadaver, and the blonde curls of the little one still formed a kind of halo around her face.[1]

Indeed, I never forgot this terrible story either. Nothing of the many tales of reprisals, torture, and killings I heard in contact after contact with the FFI had brought home the true reality of the war as did this slaughter of innocents. By the time the reality of the death camps, of Auschwitz, Buchenwald, Maideneck and all the rest was established as incontrovertible fact, I needed no confirmation. The Nazi terror in France was but a prelude to the enormity of what had been wherever Hitler's arms and men went in the east. The "terrorists" were babes in arms, the paralyzed, the young, the old, any and everyone so labelled, and so any and all atrocities were not just permissible: they were encouraged and prepared with Teutonic thoroughness and efficiency, as in the Final Solution.

Among documents extant are the notes of an interview between the French prefect of the *départemente* of Indre-et-Loire, Monsieur Fernand Russo, and Lieutenant Colonel Stenger of the Feldkommandandantur 788 of Tours concerning the massacre. The latter writes his regrets and disavows responsibility for the events that took place. He asserts that he tried to stop the killings once he was informed of the matter, but by then, it was too late to do anything. Fifty-two of sixty homes had been destroyed and 124 people killed.

Charges were brought against the officer responsible for the crimes of homicide in Maillé. His name was Gustav Schlueter. He was a second lieutenant. He was born in Kiel, Germany, on June 2nd, 1907 and had been a traveling salesman before the war. By the time the Military Tribunal of Bordeaux had brought charges against Schlueter on January 31st, 1952, the accused had completely disappeared. Another charge was brought against Schlueter in 1972 for contempt of court. The judgment against the accused was unanimous in condemning him for the murders of the inhabitants of Maillé and for having organized such killings and ordered them to be carried out.

Sentenced to death for his crimes, Gustav Schlueter was never found. His last known address was Langenhorn 1–159 Stockflethiveg, Hamburg, Germany.

Half a century after the massacre, Maillé is once again a quiet, pleasant village. The rebuilding began in 1946. Help came in part from the United States. An American couple from Santa Barbara, California, Gerard and Kathleen Hale, said they wanted to "adopt" the martyred village. They generously sent all sorts of goods, from kitchen pots to blankets and clothing, for the survivors. They took children to Paris, and continued a close relationship with Maillé until 1958, after which no more news of the Hales was received.

No one in Maillé has forgotten the events of August 25th, 1944, however. The victims' graves in the nearby cemetery are decorated with fresh flowers. On Sundays the mayor, Monsieur Gilbert Chedozeau, is in the rebuilt city hall to talk with visitors who have come to see the modest but deeply moving exhibit of the massacre. The Abbé Payon, seriously ill and living in Tours while still alive, was barely able to shake my hand when I saw him after fifty years. A plaque was recently dedicated in the village to his memory. His story, the story of the terrible events that took place in Maillé, and the flaming omelette he made for us in Dombasle in the fall of 1944, were things one does not easily forget.

Notes

1. From Payon's book on the massacre: Abbé André Payon, Curé de La Celle-Saint-Avant, Drache et Maillé. *Maillé martyre*. Tours: Arrault et Cie., 1945. Through the good offices of Christian Couppé, I was able to get a copy of the original publication on its wartime paper.

   A new book, on far better paper but based primarily on information in the Abbé's book, has been published by Paul de Lagalussière: *Le massacre de Maillé*, Montreuil-Bellay: Editions C.M.D., 1994. There is also *En Touraine, Je me souviens. Maillé*, a small volume edited by the Conseil Général d'Indre-et-Loire on the commemoration of the fiftieth anniversary of the massacre. Of particular interest is the inclusion of photos of documents of the period relating to the event, full listing of names of the victims, and the name of the German officer.

   The passages in English are my translations from the Abbé's book of 1945 which contains extensive photographs of the victims, of the destruction, and of the ceremonies of burial that took place on September 17th, 1945.

   Abbé André's parents died some years ago, but we corresponded for many years after the war. André, his brother Hubert had told me, had had a very serious operation, and lived in Tours.

XVII

THE DAY RALPH and I drove away from Dombasle, Madame Payon came running down the main street holding out her arms to us. She was crying, and I had tears in my eyes too. We had formed a deep bond, that family and I, as I did also with the other families we had gotten to know and who had treated us with such warmth. Now things were going to change. Going east from Dombasle, we were heading into those areas of Lorraine which, like all of Alsace, had been declared a part of Germany as soon as Hitler's hordes had moved in.

We were driving into the dark corners of the land where sullen people looked on us with suspicion. These were the German-speaking people in the annexed territories. The "Germanization" had been swift and ruthless. All highly placed French officials were replaced by Germans. The lesser bureaucrats were forced to sign a statement declaring their adherence to the annexation to Germany and to the Fuhrer. Otherwise they were expelled into France proper. They were permitted to take one valise and a small sum of money with them. Everything else was confiscated.

As early as mid July, the mayors of every city and town received a list of undesirables. At the head of the list, as might be expected, were the Jews. Those who had not been evacuated before the Nazi arrival were forced to clean the streets every day until they were loaded on trucks, the old, the ill, the infirm as well as those in good health, for transportation into France itself. German statistics give a figure of 22,000 persons thus driven from their homes.[1]

The undesirables were not confined to the Jews, however. All Frenchmen from other parts of France, francophile Alsacians, all veterans of the Spanish Civil War who had fought for the Republican forces, Gypsies, foreigners, common criminals, and "anti-social" persons. All were to be deported for the purity of the new Nazi territories.

The Christians sometimes fared almost as badly as the Jews. The cathedral of Strasbourg was offered to the Protestants, who refused to take it over. Consequently, it was to become a war museum. Great numbers of priests were deported, some into France, others to concentration camps. The Gestapo set up block control of the population, labor was forced when enough volunteers did not come forth. Statues of Jeanne d'Arc were destroyed, as were those memorials to the dead of World War I. Statues of Goethe were put up instead, and the swastika on flag, banner and armband was seen everywhere.

French was replaced by German everywhere also. People were forbidden to speak French. Penalties for doing so were severe. This was the land we now entered into, not far in miles from that sunny Loire valley of August, but enormously distant in clime and ambience. Here there was no cheering, no welcome. Just the sullen faces of people who expressed their fears and resentment at their checkered history and who saw themselves as chattels of both the

French and the Germans over decades. Those who spoke French did so with an accent so thick as to be almost incomprehensible. I had to rely on what little German I had learned from my little *Hier Spricht Man Deutsch* book from Dombasle.

The Maginot Line was just ahead of us, that vast underground line of defense that had defended nothing. Just beyond it was the Maginot's counterpart, the Siegfried Line. At any rate, the Germans were no longer running from us. They were prepared for us. Night after night, artillery duels took place.

In Morhange, then still Mörchingen, we took over what must have been a kind of office for the former Nazi administrators. Our predecessors had left us a delightful present, a huge portrait of Hitler in full color. We quickly cut it to pieces, not recognizing in it a memento that we probably would have been wiser to keep. Our quarters were in a yard back of an apartment house. Nearby was a filthy latrine that all of us had to use, and underneath the house was a basement that had been reinforced against bombardment, by air or by artillery. Our planes had bombed the town on Armistice day, leaving whole sections in flames, another reason for a decided lack of warmth toward us.

Headquarters for XII Corps was set up in an old barracks in Morhange from November 23rd until December 8th. The building had served both French and German troops over the years as the town changed hands. Now it was housing Americans, as was a large school building. By then, the Germans were sending buzz-bombs into the area and extensively utilizing time bombs and land mines. They were also using the railway gun that had shelled Nancy. It was figured that the range used for Morhange was some 16 miles. The combination made for little sleep and the need to pay attention to where we walked or drove.

By this time, any kind of protection from the cold, the rain, and the snow, was a luxury. So was hot food. Our two teams had made arrangements for us to be fed in a sort of dingy restaurant where we could at least have some hot food prepared from our rations. The women who worked there were short-tempered and complaining, but what they prepared for us hardly matched the sometimes memorable transformation of rations earlier was better than eating directly out of cans. One day, however, our "benefactors" said they would no longer serve us. One of the women's husbands had been arrested by the new French authorities for collaborating. It was up to us to get the man out of prison or go without hot meals. The blackmail worked. After all, every resident in Morhange had *had* to collaborate in order to survive, hadn't they? They had no choice. We solemnly nodded in agreement, figuring the French could settle their scores after we had moved on. We interfered, and the cooks carried on.

Our little barracks office, uncomfortable as it was, was also better than being out in the open. We had a roof over our heads at night and an earthen floor to roll out our bedding on. Close by was a cemetery and a solidly Germanic office building, both still in existence today. When the shelling began after dark, we were all in our bedrolls. I was ensconced closest to a brick wall. Palmer was next to me, and the others lined up beyond him. Everybody but Palmer and I got up and hurried across the yard to the apartment house and its basement. We were defiant. To hell with the bastards, was our comment, but we quickly changed our tune. A couple of shells came in very close, and a big section of bricks fell down within an inch or so of my head. We brushed away the dust and followed the others. There were flames shooting up over by the cemetery. Two shells had indeed come in very close. We joined the mothers and children in the shelter. Next night, we got up automatically, after the first shelling. Bastards they were, and aiming fairly accurately at us.

From Morhange, XII Corps moved east to what was left of the little town of Puttelange. No restaurant there, not even a dingy one. We stood in the rain with our messkits for food or opened K-rations. The place and our situation was grim. We had no inkling, of course, that the Germans were preparing their last major offensive, thereby thrusting Third Army into its fiercest and most heroic battles. We were in the land of the enemy, after all. People spoke of *gauleiters* rather than mayors when we asked about officialdom. Hardly reassuring.

One such official was fingered as a real Nazi. He had been the local *gauleiter*. He lived on a farm outside the town, and I was to interrogate him. I and one of the CIC men drove into the countryside until we came to the road leading to the farm. It was mined, we had been told, so I got out and walked by myself some two miles to the farmhouse where the supposedly formidable *gauleiter* lived. I was ready for tragedy, but instead ended up with comedy.

Like most of the farms in the region, one side of the house was for the cattle and the other for the human beings. I was a bit apprehensive as I was ushered into the kitchen by what I took to be the farmer's wife. She spoke only German, no French. I sat in silence wondering if this was a ploy so that our official could not be questioned or arrested. I soon found out. The farmer himself came in and briefly but patiently explained that he needed help. His cow was giving birth to a calf. Können Sie helfen? Ya, Ich kann. And so, instead of being the fearful interrogator, I became a midwife. We delivered a frisky, if wobbly, calf. My reward was a couple of good snorts of Schnapps and many a danke schön.

Neither the man nor his wife had an appearance of being fire-spitting Nazis. I had shot my wad as far as German was concerned, and so walked back down the road to my comrade and jeep a bit wiser in matters of anatomy if no wiser concerning the politics of this benighted area! I left, convinced that this was hardly a man for our authorities to fear. Why had we been led to believe that? A settling of accounts, as the French would have put it? But by whom and for what reason?

Our intelligence teams, by then scattered as needed throughout the area, moved on towards the Saar and Germany proper. We shaved in our helmets, and washed in our helmets. We had no bath or shower for days at a time. The mud was everywhere. No privileged lodgings for us there. We stood for chow, messkits in hand, in the rain and sleet like any other GI, but we were lucky enough to be able to put our bedrolls inside shelter, whether with heat or not. We did not envy those in pup-tents outside. The tents of the artillery men had small dikes around them to keep out the water and mud that was everywhere by now. And the guns were very active.

The eve of my birthday, December 12th, was a particularly noisy one, with artillery firing through the night. We were in the shelter of a house, empty of furniture except for a bedstead with springs and an iron stove for heating, its owners huddled in the basement in fear. We fired up the stove and spent a warm night. The only problem was the shells. With each one, I awakened, flames dancing on the ceiling like a Bosch painting of hell. The next morning, we drove under a pale winter sun on to Saarguemines. The town's farther side was taken that very morning of December 13th, and there were still snipers and gunners in the city, and artillery batteries just beyond. Our welcome was the sight of medics carrying litters with two dead GIs out of the town's city hall.

It was, however, my birthday, and one of the CIC men found a wine cellar with huge barrels of wine, fully intact. That meant two reasons for celebration, and the where-withal to do so. Ralph Palmer recalled recently that "Joe Flanagan was the one sitting on top of the wine keg in Saarguemines, a siphon in one hand and a gun in the other, shouting, 'Keep away you bastards it's mine.' We emptied all the water cans and filled them with wine. The next day I shaved with wine – no water available."[2] Several of us decided to take a stroll around town, but gave up on it when we were nearly machine-gunned going around a corner. Instead, we settled on a spin along the river out into the country. The wine had given us considerable courage. The artillery gunners at an emplacement by the river that we drove out to told us we were the only jeep to get that far without being fired on. We replied that it was drinkers' luck.

That night, an artillery duel went on over our heads, our artillery on one high point of the town, the Germans on the other. The shells whistled past the little Hotel Ganser where we had our beds unrolled. In the morning, a jeep pulled up and the driver asked for me. Our French-speaking team was to head back into France. In a sense, my birthday marked the end of our usefulness. We were the French speakers. The German interrogation teams were now to take over.

For several days we stayed in the area of the Maginot Line. After that we headed to that Paris I so yearned to see. When we drove into the city in the late afternoon, we were amazed to see Americans in clean uniforms, with shining boots and metal. Intelligence headquarters was in the suburb of Le Vésinet, to the west of Paris on the Seine River, but all of us wanted to wait until the next morning, the 17th, to report in. We stopped in a small hotel not far from the Gare St. Lazare where we too could bathe and shave and spruce up like civilized beings.

Meanwhile, I phoned Neuilly, where the de Nervo and de la Gravière family from Vendôme lived. I was quickly invited to have my first Paris meal at their home. The Métro was working until midnight, so out I went. Despite the shortages, we ate well and drank well. A lengthy friendship thus began. Like Cinderella, I caught the last Métro back into the center of the city, and slept soundly through the dropping of two bombs on nearby Gare St. Lazare. It was the night of December 16th. Hitler's final offensive was under way, the savage Battle of the Bulge. Third Army and XII Corps were in the thick of it, but it was not until we got to Le Vésinet that we heard about what was happening.

By next morning when we arrived at Les Ibis at Military Intelligence headquarters, there was a kind of chaos. Rumors had gotten around that the Germans were planning to parachute men into the Paris area. There was considerable talk of issuing firearms to everybody for protection. Some of our unseasoned fellows at headquarters, we laughingly decided, would be a greater danger armed than any parachutists the Germans might drop. The next day, however, our Team 443 was in our jeeps heading north into the region from which we so recently had come.

As we grew closer to the battle areas, we found that road signs had been torn down or turned around. It made finding directions very difficult. This was to confuse Germans, we knew, but it confused us as well. We had quite a time finding out where we were to go. At several points Military Police stopped us and questioned us to be certain we were Americans and not English-speaking Germans in American uniforms. Fortunately, some of my comrades were better informed about baseball than I was. If I had had to answer some of the questions, we probably would have ended up shot by our own GIs.

Our CIC unit, we finally learned, was in Luxembourg City. We joined it there. Battles were raging all around, and artillery could be heard in the distance. Concerned that the Germans might return and take reprisals had led many a shopkeeper to take down the welcome signs in English, but soon the city itself took on an eerie air of peacetime normalcy. It was just before Christmas, and astonishingly enough there was food in shop windows, even ham and pickles, as well as pastries! We were not supposed to buy anything of the sort, but the sight of such splendors was heartwarming after the many months of seeing only drab or empty shops. It seemed like a ray of hope of better times to come.

That Christmas Eve, we sang carols, and ignored the air raid sirens. Then, mission truly over, as was the Bulge thanks to the heroism of so many men of Third Army, we left active participation in the war behind us. We had been in the Battles of Normandy, Northern France, the Rhineland, and the Ardennes.

I later calculated that I had participated in the interrogations of something like 7000 to 8000 people, Frenchmen, laborers, officials, clergy, workers, whoremasters, students, farmers, shopkeepers, officers and enlisted men of our army and of the French or the British, every level of the social spectrum, from titled nobility to the cleaning woman of a brothel. On one single morning in Lorraine I interrogated 473 men and women who had been forced into the infamous Organization Todt of the Nazis. Early in 1945 I wrote home:

> I have worked on interrogations when I was tired and have had to knot my muscles physically to squeeze enough energy not just to speak French but also to appear alert to my victim, to play with him mentally, to try to trick him in his statements, maybe to browbeat him, intimidate him, be confidential and friendly, do anything at all to get information from him or probe his mind to see if counter-intelligence was interested. I enjoyed that when I felt good, but that went on every single day, without one Sunday or holiday, sometimes until 2 and 3 in the morning, for about six months.[3]

In those interrogations, we used no torture, but we did humiliate, and we did turn people over to the FFI. We knew of arrests, even of shootings, which be it said to our credit we did try to prevent. I myself watched French

196

police mercilessly beat an accused blackmarketeer. As officers took turns across the room, I sat with the others smoking and talking, pretending not to hear or see what was going on.

In my experience, we Americans were always treated with respect, but our own officers and men often saw the French as inferior to us. They all too frequently acted as though they were dealing with the enemy rather than with friends. This could greatly complicate our job as interpreters. Officers would give orders to local officials with a demeanor we had supposed would be kept for the Germans. French pride was sometimes deeply wounded. Misunderstandings were frequent. I soothed feelings. I listened, I saw, and I learned. Instead of translating "tell that SOB" or "tell that bastard such and such," I would water things down, shake hands and use "monsieur" to the French official, with a smile rather than a scowl.

For a nation of immigrants, American insularity was as astonishing then as it is now. Foreigners were foreigners, whether friend or foe, German or French, anyone not American. Of course, most GIs didn't think of *themselves* as foreigners, even in the foreigners' own land. The French didn't speak our language, they ate different food, and they were definitely strange, that is, foreign, even in France! I usually handled it pretty well, and avoided conflict or bad feeling. The French were our allies. That did occur to me, but I was in the minority.

Notes

1. Statistics are from *La France occupée 1940–1941*, a collection of articles with numerous photographs, published by Editions Tallandier in 1979.

197

2. Letter from Ralph Palmer dated January 22nd, 1993.
3. From a letter sent to my family in Columbus, Ohio, dated from Paris, January 22nd, 1945.

XVIII

I T TOOK TWENTY years to get me back to
Utah Beach for the first time. It was in the
summer of 1964. I drove out with close friends
from Paris, Paul Bougenaux and his wife Lucille. Paul, a
youthful Resistance fighter and member of the Maquis
during the Occupation, eventually became chief concierge
and then director of the Hotel Plaza Athenée in Paris.
We met while I was studying in France after the war, and I
was a witness at the Bougenauxs' wedding on January 21st,
1948.

My first return to France had been in the fall of 1947.
The old SS *De Grasse* had been refurbished by the French
and made into what (as far as I know) was the world's
first two-class transatlantic liner. It was, I was told, the
first passenger ship back in service between Europe and
America. I took it in mid-September, tourist class of course,
accompanied by a surprising number of French-speaking
Canadians more or less my age. War was certainly on no
one's mind as we made a delightfully pleasant crossing.
The weather could not have been better, we sunned on the
deck, danced in the lounge and had very good food, and,
being a French ship, wine. After all, the hit song the
orchestra played over and over was *Oh Le Petit Vin Blanc*.
We sang it and we drank it. In the dining room, we noted

that the English ate singularly large portions. We had all heard of the severe rationing they were returning to. We were soon to face considerable restrictions in France ourselves. That was war's heritage. Europe had to live with it for quite a while.

I was forewarned about the acute shortages I would find. Everyone I consulted before the trip told me to be prepared: the black market flourished. Take cigarettes, take a radio, take any kind of electronic equipment, and take *dollars*. I did all of that, but had also been warned about taking in very *many* dollars. I hid some in the bottom of a deodorant jar. I also had letters of introduction to Alice B. Toklas and Constantin Brancusi.

Once in Paris, a friend from Ohio who worked at our Embassy invited me to have a drink at the English Bar of the Plaza Athenée, a very ritzy place to go. The young bartender was Paul Bougenaux. Shortly after our first meeting, he invited me and my fellow Buckeye to dinner at his brother and sister-in-law's house to meet his fiancée, Lucille.

It was the beginning of a friendship that continued throughout the years, despite my gaffe at that evening's dinner. Soup was served as a first course, when Paul asked me if I liked brains. Having earned my lunch and date money throughout high school as a grocery boy, the idea of eating those quavering blood-spotted membranes filled me with loathing. I expressed my horror at the thought, but soon realized that I was undoubtedly doomed to consuming the detestable cranial innards.

Glad we decided on sweetbreads, said Paul. But by then I knew. I determined to eat brains, come hell or high water, and managed to smile happily as the quivering mound covered with white sauce was placed before me. I even had seconds of "those delicious sweetbreads," to everyone's obvious amusement. Several days later, when we met on the street, friend Paul told me what a laugh the family had had: the laugh's on you, I explained. I *knew* I was eating brains. It was the first and last time.

By 1964, of course, France had rebuilt and was prosperous. We could see where new structures had been built on the foundations of what was left from the war, and it was hard to envisage what the Norman towns we passed through had been like twenty years before.

Our target on our summer trip that year was not Utah Beach, however. That was a kind of second thought. "Would you like to go by Utah Beach?" Paul casually asked me. It wouldn't be far out of the way.

Actually, Paul was taking us to Mont Saint Michel. I never forgot seeing it in the distance as our jeep went south from Avranches over the bridge of Pontaubault. Finally I was going to visit it. Our minds were not on battlefields but on the famous abbey and on rich hearty Norman food washed down by a spot of Calvados, the famous *"trou normand"* that clears the system of fatty substances, or so the explanation goes. By then the war, although in a sense ever present in me, seemed far behind. Like most veterans, I tried to erase the memories as we scurried about getting our lives going in the terrifying nuclear world of the Cold War.

Our first stop was at the casino in Deauville for a bit of gambling, then on to the Port-en-Bassin where the Impressionists painted. Our modest hotel was known for its lobster dish, *homard à l'armoricaine* (also often called erroneously *à l'américaine*). We joyously overate. The next day began

201

with a visit to Bayeux to see the famous tapestry of Queen Matilda and then on across the Peninsula to the famous towering medieval monastery, every bit as exciting as the guide books claimed. There, in addition to a *trou* of the famous monument, we had the traditional *omelette bavante*, the "slobbering omelet," of la Mère Poularde, followed by the lamb chops flavored by the pastures of salt marshes in the area. It was a holiday and Paul, with customary largesse, wanted me to see and enjoy it all.

The stop at Utah Beach seemed perfunctory. We were the only visitors. By then, there was a modest museum by the main breach in the tank wall through which the vehicles had streamed from June 6th on. When I told the lady at the entrance to the little museum that I had landed there in July of 1944, she flatteringly said that I looked far too young. I smiled and assured her that, yes, I had landed there, but not through the break in the wall to one side of the museum.

She assured me that I *had* come through there. I *had* to. In the meantime, Paul and Lucille, as sated as I from our sumptuous lunch and perhaps wiser than I, decided to take a nap in the car. I set out to explore.

The beach was empty. It was hard to imagine it as it had been in July 1944, with ships as far as the eye could see, with ramps out into the water, landing craft coming and going disgorging men and vehicles. I strolled along and, lo, before I knew it, there was the other break in the fortifications. Madame was wrong; I was right. *That* was where I had gone through, the first of my team to set foot in France and ironically also the first to skirt death at the very outset before I could do even that.

If that stop at the landing beach was relatively un-emotional, the walk in Colleville military cemetery was

202

a different matter. I had crossed the Channel on a Liberty ship on a hot and gloriously clear July day. We had stripped to the waist and sunbathed about the deck. As we neared the shores of France, we were staggered at the number of ships on either side of us. Then as evening came on, we stayed on deck to watch the display of artillery and the dogfights in the distance. It was like some huge fireworks display that someone had staged for our arrival.

The next morning, rain squalls followed bright sunshine. That I had remembered, or thought I remembered. It seemed so strange that I thought my memory had played tricks on me. That morning in the cemetery, however, there in those rows of crosses with the occasional Star of David, the sun and the showers followed one another, as though some force wanted to remind me that all of that was not frivolity.

The visit to the graves was a deeply moving moment. We wept openly, wept for those who had died and suffered and those who lived on, changed and wounded in body or in spirit by what had happened in those years. But what point was there to returning to that silent beach? It was as dead as the person I had been twenty years earlier.

Ten years after that, there was another bit of tracking down of time past. It took place during a trip to France in 1974 made for professional reasons, to check out Ohio Wesleyan's student program in Segovia, Spain, and to see how things were going with the French program we shared with Otterbein College in Dijon in France. It was February. Spain was cold, and France was even colder. There was rain, snow, and sleet in Segovia, snow and ice in Dijon.

Back in Ohio, I gave some chilly replies to such jolly remarks as "How was sunny Spain?"

I made a detour from Dijon up to Nancy, rather than directly back to Paris to catch my return flight home. I had been able to get in contact with one of my good friends from 1944, one of the only ones with whom I had maintained contact, and we felt that after thirty years it was time to resume that friendship.

I visited Mimi Gallien and met his wife. We had not seen each other since we had worked together in Dombasle. I was excited at the prospect, but also hoped to see the Place Stanislas, the old Hotel Theirs across from the station where we had been billeted, and, not least of all, going to back to Dombasle.

On the train from Epinal, an elderly couple began talking with me. They were much like the elderly couple I had chatted with when I first began studying French. They proudly showed off photographs of a daughter married and living in Toronto and offered to share their bread, wine, and home-made paté with me. Outside, the passing countryside had the look of the north-eastern part of France I had known in the fall of 1944. Fields, thickets, woods, small rivers, all cloaked in grey. They asked me if I would lend them some money. They were short of francs. I agreed to lend them some, and did get it back later on by mail.

When the train pulled into the Nancy station, there was Mimi awaiting me. No problem of identification. We knew each other right away. We had not seen each other for thirty years, but we excitedly exclaimed on how little we had aged!

Mimi and I had corresponded every year at Christmas

time for quite a while. He was living with and supporting his mother. When she died, however, Mimi married and moved. We lost touch, until a letter from me was forwarded to his new address in a suburb of Nancy, Laxou. It was there we drove to his home for a memorable meeting with his wife Paule and daughters Christine and Claudie, and, of course, a dinner that began with champagne and ended with one of my favorite Lorraine *eaux-de-vie*, Mirabelle. There was a Lorraine torte, roast chicken, salad, and a special Lorraine cake, plus quantities of wine to wash it all down. Delicious and delightful, until the morning after!

Daughter Claudie was studying German and English. She showed me two poems in English that were surprisingly good. She was interested in visiting the States, and the following summer an exchange did take place. Ohio Wesleyan chaplain's daughter Diane was studying French, was the same age as Claudie, and was very happy at the prospect of spending time in France. Claudie duly came to Delaware, Ohio, and Diane went to Nancy.

Mimi remembered Ralph Palmer, but by then I had lost sight of him. We talked of him as we drove down to Dombasle, and I dutifully jotted in my notebook on the express to Paris:

Yesterday afternoon, Mimi took me back to Dombasle to see the house where I lived with the Payons, now dead, and the Solvay Amicale where I had my office. We even went past the "point" where we crawled through the bushes with guns ready, night after night in the rain, finding, of course, nothing. Also up to the workers' district where Giselle lived, and by the Audoyers' house.

That was just an afternoon's visit. We saw no one and made no contacts with anyone before going back to Nancy to see where we had had our offices on the Place Stanislas. A *real* return to Dombasle seemed impossible. I wondered if I would ever go back. After all, thirty years had gone by since Ralph and I made our daily rounds by jeep through towns, villages, and countryside.

XIX

WITH THE approach of the 50th anniversary of D-Day and the onslaught against Fortress Europa, many a veteran remembered that bitter-sweet September song so plaintively sung by Walter Houston, oh, so many years ago ... the days dwindling down to a precious few, the autumn weather, leaves turning to flame, and so little time for the old waiting game. Old soldiers do die, and with them the nostalgia for youth, the joys and miseries of first love, the hopes for so many things, our stories of war. The time had come. Fish or cut bait.

The trip of 1991 reinforced my feelings about this. The interview with Raymond Casas took place right by the bridge over the Loire that had been blown up by the Germans a bit before our two jeeps drove into town. It was the spur, like Proust's little cake, that began the remembrance of time past, the 1944 of my experience. The wealth of material that I began to mine in the summer of 1992 and the two following summers was far richer than anyone could have imagined.

On the trip with the Grabers in 1991, we had stayed at the Grandins' near Utah Beach. By then, the small museum at the main landing point had doubled in size. In front of the building were landing barges, tanks, signs, and nearby, monuments, plaques, and flags flying in the wind. The displays and film were very well done. We drove on, first to Point du Hoc which is singularly impressive, then to the American cemetery. The visit there was as deeply moving as it had been years before. Our next stop, the port of Arromanches, was totally changed, however. In the winter of 1945 when Pierre Lenoir and I had gone there to recover abandoned equipment, it was an abandoned village with its port of sunken vessels still intact. By the 1990s, its sunken ships had been removed for sale as scrap. Only the caissons remained. A part of history had been sacrificed to practicality. The beaches were full of tourists, not GIs. And the town which then had been totally empty was now jammed with cars and people. I had distinct inklings I was turning into a dinosaur.

Our next stay-over was in another *chambre d'hôte* or *gîte* to the south of Tours on the Cher River at Savonnière. Another excellent experience, this time in a house dating from the fifteenth century. The owner graciously offered to phone Blois for a *gîte* for the next night. It turned out to be at Les Grouëts on the Loire, a short distance outside the city of Blois itself. The owners were Monsieur and Madame Yves Cosson. Another first-rate place. When we arrived, I did not know or even intuit what an impact staying at that home would have on my life. It was a turning point.

It came about very simply. Madame Cosson asked me if I had ever been to Blois before. I answered that I had and then told her the story of the night of September 16th, 1944, when the two jeeploads of us came down from Vendôme. Madame quickly said that she had friends who had been in the Resistance who would be very interested to hear my story. Hardly said than done, she began making some phone calls, and by the next day I had three visitors, Madame Jeanne Madeleine Jacob, the president of the *Société France-Etats-Unis*, a society of friendship between France and the United States, a reporter from the local newspaper, *La Nouvelle République*, and last, but surely not least, one Christian Couppé, amateur World War II buff, who as I have said before, was central to the ensuing experience of recapturing Patton's race across France half a century ago.

The next day, I was to be interviewed for the paper by a reporter and Resistance leader, Raymond Casas. The latter also was to become a very helpful friend whose writings about the Occupation and the Resistance movement, and whose encyclopedic knowledge, have been a source of much information. I was also to be interviewed, with Madame Jacob, at the local radio station. The Jacobs had a cocktail party for us to meet an American naval officer of the war, Jim Lemire, formerly of Massachusetts, and his French wife, Marie Louise, one of the most decorated women of the Resistance. In the space of three days, important and lasting friendships were formed. I felt something of the astonishment an eighteenth-century archeologist must have experienced on digging up the first fragment of a mural at Pompeii. Who could have believed such a thing? I was on the way back into that faraway world to an extent I only fully realized the following summer.

I recovered a yellowing address book with names and places of people met in 1944. It proved to be a valuable source for tracking people down. The marvelous French invention of the Minitel with its computer screen also proved invaluable. Christian Couppé began reporting to me by phone and letter that he had located this person and that. By the time we went back to Blois the summer of 1992, there were all sorts of people to meet.

That August, we took our time going north from Spain. There were just the two of us, Fran and I. We headed up through central France to the Berry region, particularly to see the home of Georges Sand at Nohant, as I had written about her work. From there we stopped in the cathedral city of Bourges before going to Blois on the appointed day of August 9th. Although Christianne Couppé, Christian's wife, had never met us, we were welcomed like members of the family into their home, and there we stayed throughout the ceremonies of the liberation in three of the cities where I had gone just after XII Corps was activated.

The first ceremony took place in Vendôme on Tuesday, August 11th. On the way, we drove with Dr. Raymond and Madame Janou Jacob, and Christian to Colommiers-la-Tour. After forty-eight years, I was about to revisit Huchigny, the country estate of Viscount Hubert Jurien de la Gravière. In that lovely country home I had dined with him, his wife Claude, sister-in-law Monique de Nervo, and baby daughter Sylvine. That was a part of the Vendôme legacy.

The Sylvine I had held as a baby and her husband, Gonzages de Geloes, and two of their children gathered about as we sipped champagne on the terrace and talked about the long-ago meeting. From there to meet the Count and Countess Michel de Rochambeau and their son Guy, and to see memorabilia of their famous ancestor, before going into Vendôme itself for the ceremonies.

A surprising number of people attended. Couppé had had a poster made up of the photo I had sent him of myself with several youngsters taken on August 14th. Two of the "boys" came to the ceremonies, one walking with a cane. At the reception following the more formal wreath-laying and official speeches, several hundred people came to talk with me, touch my hand, and to ask me to sign the poster-photograph for them and their children. Many had tears in their eyes as they told of what the liberation had meant to them and to their families. It was a deeply moving experience, as were those ceremonies to follow. Pierre de Saint Céran, one of the resistance leaders at the banquet in Vendôme in 1944, participated. We reminisced and re-established our friendship.

In St. Calais, on the road from Le Mans to Vendôme, the wartime photo brought a response from the little tow-headed boy who stood beside me that noonday. He was Guy Chesneau, now with his wife, Paulette. The newspaper article about that re-encounter was entitled "The Boy Refinds His Soldier." We did meet Nicole, now Madame Alain Blu, the baby sister I had held in my arms, with all her family later on. That day we also saw the impressive new library, and stopped at Montoire on the way home so that Raymond Casas could show us the railway station of the much-publicized meeting between Marshal Pétain and Hitler.

The Blois ceremony was even more elaborate than the other two. Paul Huger from Vendôme, who had driven us about in his carefully restored American jeep, vintage 1944, was on hand, as were several other jeep owners, plus the proud owner of a Third Army truck. We drove through the streets with the American flag streaming beside us as people gathered and applauded. We relit the flame to the martyrs of the Resistance, listened with tears

211

in our eyes as the national anthems were solemnly played, and then in jeeps and cars went to the City Hall for speeches, a champagne reception attended by some 200 persons, and a television interview. I was given three medals, all accepted as a representative of XII Corps, Third Army, and was amazed at the newspaper, television, and radio coverage of these events.

The rest of my experience with Patton's Third loomed in the future. Once more, it was made possible through Christian Couppé. We set out one sunny Monday morning, April 19th, 1993, and after a stop at the home of photographer René Millet who showed us the pictures he had taken at the previous year's ceremonies, we headed through Orleans, Gien, and Sens to Chalons-sur-Marne to spend the night and search out the house of Marie Claude Grenier. The fields were bright green or yellow with colza flowers. It was cool, but delightfully sunny, as though to compensate for the evil weather of the time of war.

Marie Claude was no longer alive, but the owner of the house invited me to come in to that home where we had had that Sunday afternoon party and sung Charles Trenet songs. We drove about Bar-le-Duc, now doing some major restoration of its oldest quarters, before heading to Nancy and Laxou for a reunion lunch with Mimi and Paule Gallien. Another memorably pleasant meal, with reminiscences of the one twenty years earlier when both daughters were still at home.

That night we drove on to Lunéville where I recounted to Christian for the umpteenth time his favorite story of my finding myself driving my jeep just behind Patton's as we both headed, on some sort of business, towards the chateau. I slowed down considerably, making certain

Patton was out of sight and I out of range before walking into the building before which we both parked. There was the fabled "boss" all right, with boots shining like a mirror, and driver equally meticulously outfitted. I was properly attired, but who would want to risk a demerit or worse from the General himself?

The next day was a full one with members of the Resistance from Dombasle. The people of Lorraine have a reputation for being unfriendly to strangers, a reputation wholly unmerited if my experience is any proof. Jean Césard, Pierre Ballé, Raymond Grimm, and René Fresse took me through the Solvay building where Ralph and I had had our office, where we had interrogated the man with the injured foot, and the dark-haired Raymonde had possibly riffled through our files. We went into the country-side to the site where arms had been hidden and a monument is going up, to a luncheon in an inn, joined by Claude Wrobel, and wandered through the streets of the town where I had known people and where I had lived with the Payons. There was a ceremony, a medal presentation by Mayor Robert Blaise, and a reception at which Gérard Berge and Michel Caps interviewed me for the local paper.

The next morning, we backtracked to Toul where we spent the morning talking with Michel Hachet of the municipal museum and seeing the excellent collection of war memorabilia. From there, we walked to the house of Dr. Rhotan, and past the house of Dr. Gregoire before driving back to Nancy for lunch with Hubert and Mimi Payon. As I have said, Brother André, the writer of the book on the massacre of Maillé, seriously ill, was still alive in Tours. Efforts to talk with him personally did not work out, except for a very brief meeting, but reminiscing about

213

the famous dinner party with Hubert and Mimi was touching for us all.

The final part of the journey took us to Morhange, where the caretaker of the retirement village that replaced the apartment building and little school where we had slept showed us around and shared stories of the war with us. Then on to Saarguemines, so changed it was unrecognizable, but where by sheer accident we stayed at the modest Hotel Deux Etoiles, the former Hotel Ganser where we had our bedrolls the night of my birthday, December 13th, 1944, and whose owner gave me a key ring from the old German hotel as a souvenir.

I had forgotten how lovely the center of Luxembourg perched above its great ravine is, especially in the early spring when we went back. A photo of December 24th shows me accoutered with heavy coat and helmet in hand. We took another photograph in the exact spot. I had put on weight.

We decided to go on to Bastogne, ate on the little square where a tank serves as a reminder of the ferocious fighting which centered on the town, and to the great monument to the Americans in the nearby countryside. The war museum is impressive. Its collection of war vehicles is astonishing. I was the only American there that day, but there were a lot of Germans discussing their own imposing vehicles.

Being so close, it seemed imperative to go on to Verdun and the battlefields of World War I. They themselves have become a huge museum. Brush and trees have grown in and around the trenches and outpost, but there they are in the churned land where the shells exploded and the slaughter ran into the millions. Above them and the great cemetery rises the ossuary where the bones of the unknown, enemy or friend, have been gathered as a grisly reminder that has done so little to temper men's belligerencies. If much of the destruction of World War II has been physically erased, the horrors men were subjected to on those battlefields seem very real still today. Every war-monger should be forced to spend time there.

I had finally come home to my "seconde patrie," my second homeland. New friends joined the old.

XX

WITH SUCH HEADY experiences as those of 1992 and 1993 behind me, the events of the fiftieth anniversary of D-Day seemed anticlimactic. After all, I had had my celebrations. What more could I expect? Something of the D-Day "fever" did rub off on me as tours were publicized and friends asked me if we were going to participate. Indeed we were, both as veteran and as a newspaper writer.

I laughingly said that it took me a long time to become a foreign correspondent, but I did get my Associated Press card to wear alongside my veteran's 50th Anniversary of World War II badge. I was proud of both. They proved to be very convenient things to have once we got to Normandy.

The press card came through the good graces of a friend, professor emeritus of journalism at Ohio Wesleyan University and now assistant to the editor of the Delaware, Ohio, *Gazette*, Verne Edwards. Verne, fortunately for me, is a Patton buff. On the door to his office at the newspaper hangs a photo of the general in full regalia. I had the assignment of writing a series of articles on the D-Day events in June and the Liberation celebrations I had been invited to in France in August and September.

I began by writing a sort of tale of two cities in wartime,

Paris and Berlin, and of two American women, the one a heroine and the other a traitor, Josephine Baker and Mildred Gillars respectively. The latter is better known by her stage name, Axis Sally, Europe's equivalent of Tokyo Rose. How effective her broadcasts were is a matter of conjecture. I'd say zero, but she certainly had a soft voice, a persuasive line of chatter, and a wonderful collection of recordings of the Big Bands of the epoch. Her message was simply, Yankee Soldier, Go Home, This is not Your War; and then on came the music aimed at making us homesick enough to forget duty and uniform, *Deep Purple*, *In the Mood*, *I'll Be Seeing You*, *Lili Marlene*, and on and on. She did succeed in making us homesick. She did not succeed in making us desert!

Though born in Maine, Mildred Gillars was brought up in Conneat, Ohio, and was duly enrolled at Ohio Wesleyan University. Fellow alumnae remembered her as a person with a dramatic turn who liked to be "on stage." She left the university before graduating, however, went to Europe, fell in love with a German, and began her infamous broadcasts to our troops. Arrested in Berlin in 1945, Gillars was sentenced to jail for treason and served twelve years of her sentence. On her release, she returned to central Ohio where she worked and taught at a convent school. She also decided to finish her undergraduate degree at Ohio Wesleyan, and did so in 1973. Both she and the university found themselves in the spotlight, as newscasts took up the story. Veterans and their families raised a storm of protest. Gillars' degree had been erroneously reported as an "honorary" one, which of course it was not. She did march with the other graduates, fifty-one years after her original graduation date. I had met her at amateur theater activities, without knowing at first who she was. Just an ordinary person with an interest in drama, one would have said.

I had seen Baker perform in person, but never met her. The article about the two women came from conversations with Jean-Claude Baker, author of a book about his adoptive mother, *Josephine. The Hungry Heart*, and owner of Chez Josephine restaurant in Manhattan. The restaurant happily combines good French food with an ambience that recalls the famed star of the Jazz Age who was carried nude, except for a strategically decorative banana, down the great stairway on the stage of the Folies Bergères.

During the war, La Grande Josephine was an important figure in the underground in France. As a internationally known star, she was able to get travel permits to various parts of Europe where she carried out highly important and perilous intelligence missions for the Allies. Her sheet music had messages in invisible ink written on it when she went to Lisbon, for example. She was never caught, and received the highest of French military decorations after the war's end.

June 4th, 1994, was a rainy day. Christian Coupée and son Bertran had driven up from Blois to Paris to fetch us. We had coffee in our little hotel on the Quai Voltaire across from the Louvre and got on our way, first to Caen to the extraordinary museum dedicated to both world wars, and then to the Grandins' Bel Enault where several other veterans were also staying.

Fortunately, the weather cleared before the 5th when the parachute jumps were scheduled outside Ste-Mère-Eglise in memory of those parachutings of fifty years earlier. Although I had been in the airforce initially, and rejoined it at war's end, the idea of going into the parachutists, like the submarine corps, never entered my mind. I've always felt you had to be outstandingly brave to volunteer for either service, but the jump, not for me.

Other veterans, of course, did not feel the same. As we stood in a field outside the town, we watched and cheered as plane after plane disgorged its precious cargo. Only one veteran was slightly hurt. I might have had more courage after all.

D-Day plus 50 dawned with typical Normandy weather, rain and mist, and a chilling wind. We were waved through lines of French police and American MPs, my two badges working very well, and then to the bleachers set up at Utah Beach for the ceremonies. We were directed to an area with a number of empty seats, thanks to my press card. There a young sergeant asked for our "green card," which we should have received at the press tent in Ste-Mère-Eglise. I explained that we had sent faxes to the USA from there, free of charge, the day before, but had been given no card. No green card, no seat, we were told!

A very attractive lady in a raincoat standing near by came to our rescue: "Sergeant, this is a veteran with a press card. You seat him and his wife here!" "No, Mam," came the reply, "I have my orders. Without a green card, I can't seat them here." We looked at the some thirty or forty empty seats before us. The argument went on. Neither our defender nor our tormentor would give in, until finally our gracious lady called a uniformed man from another section and quietly but imperiously told him to seat us in a section across the aisle.

We were warmly welcomed and shook hands all around and were soon chatting on a first-person basis. We were also flattered to see such luminaries as Senator Glenn and other recognizable officials near by, topped off down below us with none other than the First Lady, Hillary Rodham Clinton! By the time we left and exchanged cards with our neighbors, we found we had indeed been in a VIP section. Our "buddy" Jerry was a Major General and below us and above us were members of the House of Representatives. Our kind and attractive lady had been Ambassador Pamela Harriman's executive secretary. Even the ceremonies with the two presidents, Clinton and Mitterrand, paled after that, as did receiving a medal from the mayor at Utah Beach.

For lunch we tried a restaurant at St. Côme du Mont, but it was full, and so drove on to Carentan. The small restaurant we knew about there seemed full too, but the owner called to us that he had an upstairs room with a table for us. We had barely seated ourselves when up the steps came several veterans, the last bellowing out hello to us. It was none other than Bill Montgomery, veteran medic who had gone in on D-Day and whom we knew from Los Angeles. He and his companions were the guests of Frenchman Michel Pont. The latter had gone to the local hotel and insisted that the veterans come to stay as his guests at his home. He had never forgotten the excitement as a child of seeing the Americans arrive to liberate his country, and he expressed his gratitude to as many veterans as he could.

We heard that General Patton's granddaughter Helen was in Normandy for the ceremonies, and we saw her on television. She was very approachable, one of the veterans at Le Bel Enault told us. She was staying in Néhou. We decided to drive over to try to meet her, which we did. But before being taken to where she was staying, a local man on a bicycle offered to lead us out to the field where Patton actually had had his tent. It was not far. There is a small parking area, a Sherman tank and a walk back to the orchard where newly planted apple trees are growing, thanks to the efforts of the Patton grandchildren. The monument was modest, but appropriate.

Back in the village, we were shown the manor house where the two granddaughters were staying. It was the abbey of La Flame Vivante, The Living Flame, of Regina Laudis, entrusted with the care and restoration of the grounds of the memorial in perpetuity. We first met Mother Georgina Patton, and then Helen Ayer Patton, now Mrs. Pluscyzk, and finally the Mother Abbess. It was the beginning of a warm friendship with Helen, who has made a vow to present a theatrical piece every summer in Néhou. The manor house, built in the eighteenth century and restored largely through the efforts of the two sisters, will serve as a center for work, study, and meditation, and as a focal point for remembrance of the liberation and the breakthrough which had its inception here in 1944.

That meeting was just after D-Day. On July 30th, we returned to Avranches for the liberation ceremonies to be held the following day. We assumed there would be at least one representative of the embassy there, given the importance of Avranches's pivotal location in the Patton breakthrough. At a dinner hosted by Mayor René André and Deputy Mayor Elizabeth Lucas, we found ourselves the only two Americans. We were seated with representatives from the Channel Isle of Jersey, Connétable

Robert LeBrocq, Greffier Patrick Freeley, and former Greffier Gordon Cabot and their wives. It looked as though our talk about going to the islands was to be a reality.

Given the proximity of Jersey to the Cotentin Peninsula, the presence of the Jersey group was not surprising. The attendance of an impressive delegation from Russia was less to be anticipated. The Russians were part of a trade delegation whose arrival had coincided with the Liberation ceremonies. The importance attached to this, however, could be seen in the presence of Valentin Kovalov, the vice-president of the Russian duma or parliament.

Both groups participated fully in the ceremonies the following day. It could be said that they were highly visible, but they became almost conspicuous when we found that Fran and I, one airforce veteran from North Carolina who spoke no French, and Helen Ayer Patton were representing the United States of America, and not a soul from the our embassy to celebrate this most *American* of victories! Even the German embassy sent a representative.

For the ceremony in the impressive City Hall, Robert LeBrocq wore his robe of office and an official chain of gold, silver, and enamel work that caused much admiration. Little did we know that soon it would be in our hands, and our responsibility.

The following day in Granville, we purchased a ticket to Jersey on the 7:30 ferry, with return late that afternoon. At the hotel, however, there was an urgent message to speak with the owner. She in turn explained that in the confusion of leaving, the Connétable had left the chain of office behind. He had needed it that day. Could we take it to

Jersey the next morning? I said that we already had tickets and would do so. We left the chain, worth some $40,000, in the hotel safe, picked it up the next morning and went to board our hydrofoil. To our consternation, we learned that Jersey was not a full member of the EC, and that because of that, we had to go through both security and customs check. How could we explain having that valuable chain with us? But then, we were heading toward Jersey, not away from it. We were shooed through at both ends without any problem, turned the chain over to its proper custodian, and had a delightful visit with our new-found friends and their wives.

Our arrival at Avranches had begun on a strange note. Jean-Luc Leservoisier had phoned me to tell me he had something extraordinary to share with me. He came to the hotel with papers in hand. Wasn't I from Columbus, Ohio? Had I lived on Wilson near Broad? And clearly my name was Hugh. All correct. Did I remember interrogating one W. H. Bill Turner from Columbus in 1944 as the breakthrough got under way? No, I did not. Then Jean-Luc showed me the French text. There indeed was my name in French, Hugues, and Wilson and Broad. The English, however, was somewhat different. The name of the interrogator was Hughes, the surname, and Wilson was Road, not Avenue, and Broad was Avenue, not Street, all in Columbus, but in the northern part of the city.

Dr. Ravalet, the writer of the French version of the story, came to fetch me and to tell me what had happened. Turner was a pilot of a B-24 shot down on June 10th in the vicinity of Rennes in Brittany. He was determined to get to Allied lines, and began a long and dangerous walk north in the hopes of reaching our troops in Normandy. He finally reached the area of Pontaubault where luck had it that he was put in contact with Louis Ravalet and fellow medical student Léon. The two hid Turner in a hayloft for a total of thirty-eight days, bringing him food and caring for his burns. Meanwhile, the railway bridge at Pontaubault, a scant mile from the farm, underwent increasingly intense bombing attacks. As July drew to an end, the German troop movement and the sounds of bombardment intensified.

On July 31st, Turner went to Pontaubault where he encountered American infantrymen, was put in a jeep, and taken to be interrogated as to his identity. He had no papers with him to do so, and he was still dressed in the pilot's suit he had had on since June 12th. On August 1st at Lucky Forward, a man in his mid-forties, an intelligence agent named Hughes, took Turner to mess. When Patton came in, Hughes offered to take him over to introduce him, but Turner held back. He knew how dirty and unkempt he was, and how meticulous the general was about himself and his men. He thanked Hughes, but said no, out of both fear and respect.

Hughes had been an attorney in Columbus, Ohio, in peace time, as had Turner's uncle, the two residing about a mile from each other. On his death, Turner had wanted to be buried in the American military cemetery of St. James, near Pontaubault, but the request was refused as Turner had survived the war and died at home. Ravalet, with the help of Turner's widow and daughter, did write a slender book to tell the tale, and the two men and their families remained close friends throughout all the intervening years.[1]

There are, of course, many thrilling stories of aviators

shot down and nurtured by civilians across France, but there is one more that came to light in Blois. The pilot was William Kalan, now of Weston, Massachusetts. His B-24 was part of a squadron heading for the north-western outskirts of Paris on a bombing raid. The plane was hit after crossing the Channel in the area of Rouen, but for any plane knocked out of the squadron, the instructions were to head for Switzerland or for Spain. A lone plane was an invitation for German fighters, however, and with two more engines hit, Kalan had no choice but to order his crew to bail out and to follow suit. He had dropped his bombs on an airfield as he headed south into the Loire Valley region.

Before bailing out himself, however, he saw that the plane was heading toward a large and very impressive building. It was none other than the famed Chateau of Chambord. Unknown at that time to Kalan, the chateau was the repository for the paintings of the Louvre Museum, including the celebrated Mona Lisa of Leonardo da Vinci. Even if he had known, there was nothing to do but jump, and as Kalan did so, the plane suddenly, as if by magic, veered and dove into the ground. As Kalan later said, he had almost wiped the smile off Mona Lisa's face!

Kalan had on a chest-pack parachute that would not open at first. He kept pulling the ring, but finally had to pull out the chute by hand, and had a bumpy landing. The plane had exploded in a field quite near the chateau. A young woman had been painting at the exact spot, but her father had called her to come to their little hotel near by. She lost her easel and her paints, but not her life. From the doorway where she had witnessed it all, she directed the pursuing Germans away from the forest where she had seen Kalan hide, and later helped him back to our lines. The young woman, now a handsome matron, corrected the story for us recently. She had gone out into the field because of a tiff with her new husband. The husband had called her to come in.

As I heard these and other stories of heroism and adventure, I realized how pale my own experiences had been. But there was still something that irked me. No one but Jean Deck had come forward about my arrival in Blois on the night of August 16th. People still were repeating the story of the arrival of a jeep the morning of the 17th. I decided to take the bull by the horns. I called Deck, and I called the newspaper. I asked for an interview of the two of us to be run on August 16th. If someone else who had been there was still around, I wanted to meet him. I wanted, above all, corroboration of the events as I recalled them. Couppé and Casas had confirmed my memories of the terrace without housing beyond to the river. That much was right, but what about the men of the Resistance, and particularly the one who grabbed me and saved me from a German bullet?

The interview and a large photo appeared, as I had requested, on the 16th. Although he had rarely talked about the happenings of that night, Jean Deck did at length that day. He also said that he supposed that the other comrades were dead, and that this explained the silence I had questioned. On the 17th, Deck got a phone call. It was from one Georges Fabre. We aren't all dead, came Fabre's voice. And I remember him very well. He had come bounding up onto the terrace by himself, and Charlot ran over and grabbed him. He surely wasn't very prudent.

It had taken fifty years, but I did have my eyewitness. The Blois Liberation ceremonies had been moved up to September 3rd because so many people normally were away on vacation in August. The Fabres had been away the previous Augusts when I had participated in ceremonies, but now I was to meet him. As with Jean Deck, it was a real pleasure. I could be proud of another fine friend. I learned that Charlot (Charlie) Hervé had lived in Paris after the war, but had since died. He had saved me from machine-gun or mortar fire. He and Fabre belonged to a Resistance network that included a factory making radio parts, forcibly, for the Germans. That evening, they were part of two teams of six men each assigned to protect the chateau. Fabre was the man I hoped would come forth to confirm my story that I and my three comrades had indeed been the first GIs to set foot on the soil of a liberated Blois, the evening of the 16th, *not* the morning of the 17th, and this he had now done.

Note

1. Turner's widow wrote to me after my visit with Dr. Ravalet to see the farm and the hayloft, but I learned after I had responded to her that she had died quite suddenly of a heart attack.

    The book is: W. H. Turner and Louis Ravalet. *Pontaubault 1944: Naissance d'une amitié franco-américaine.* It was printed privately by Dr. Ravalet at Fougères, 1994. A fine book about a touching friendship.

EPILOGUE

I N THAT WARTIME experience of mine, there were some very special moments, but in actuality there was far, far more grit than grin. It was considerably more than amusing incidents or encounters with hospitable Frenchmen. These may be the grist of many old-soldier reminiscences, but actually, war was living apocalyptically, like a prolonged ride on a towering roller coaster or a lung-deep drag on a cigarette. It was anticipation, fear, wondering, a unique experience, fascinating and formidable in its dehumanization. We lived on the edges of hubris and humility. Most of us had never been expendable before, flotsam in a sea of humanity, superfluous except as the tiny cog in our little machine, the military effort ... along with millions of others, civilian or military.

It must be remembered that few of us Americans at that time were professional soldiers. We grew up in the safety of our vast geographical landmass. Consequently, the very idea of participation in another world conflagration seemed unreal. We were citizens first, soldiers second, GIs in government issue (whence the term GI) from uniform to shaving kit and cigarettes, transformed somehow into one of the most effective fighting forces of history.

We did fight the epitome of evil, but we also allied ourselves to another power almost as monstrous. One almost succeeded in enslaving the world, while the other held millions of people in bondage for seven decades. Ironically, the guns barely silent, we found that our allies had become enemies, our enemies, allies.

The losses of that *good* war were colossal. The count has now moved up to approximately 60,000,000 dead. The crosses stand row on row. There we have visual reminders of where the young men in uniform have gone, but many a mass grave of men, women, the young and the old is barely marked. Today many of the same accounts are being settled in blood, leaving terrible casualties among the survivors, and destroying even more of the cultural heritage of centuries. War and massacre go steadily on. Now we can watch it in full color.

Is there a solution? Voltaire's Candide decided, after a lifetime of struggle against the horrors of his time, that there is one solution, and not a very spectacular one at that: to tend one's garden. Today we have to add, if there is any garden left to tend.

Perhaps it's simpler for a veteran just to keep in mind that we participated in the biggest war ever fought, and were lucky to do so under one of history's most colorful and successful military figures. We can take pride in that. Roland Breton never forgot one of his memorable encounters with the General. His tale epitomizes being a part of Patton's Third Army. As Breton stood watching armored vehicles roll by on a street in Avranches after the breakthrough got under way, the turret of an approaching tank opened up. There, slim and ramrod straight, stood General George S. Patton, Jr. "Breton, get that goddam helmet on," he shouted, then disappeared, as the turret closed and the line of vehicles moved on to victory.

Discipline, determination, the personal touch, and a flamboyant flair for drama: Patton's story and Third Army's remain as fascinating as ever. Patton believed in his destiny. A lot of his destiny rubbed off on his men. His destiny became ours too.

WAR MUSEUMS IN FRANCE

A S MIGHT BE expected, there is a large cluster of World War II museums in the Normandy area. They vary in size, from the modest memorial recently dedicated by Patton's granddaughters Helen and Mother Georgina just beyond Néhou, to the great memorial museum of Caen with elaborate displays of both world wars. Just driving around the Cotentin Peninsula and along its shores, one sees abandoned blockhouses and other defenses of the Germans. The cemeteries also are well worth a visit. The American ones are beautifully maintained, and they merit a visit. The cemetery where Patton lies is also well worth a trip to Luxembourg. There are also Canadian cemeteries, Franco-British cemeteries, and German cemeteries in the Normandy area. A visit to any of them is a deeply moving experience, as is one to the area around Verdun through which Third Army passed in 1944, but where the scars of the Great War are still very visible. It can easily be fitted in on the journey from the Normandy and Loire Valley area going to Luxembourg. Bastogne also has am impressive war memorial and museum just outside the city made famous during the Battle of the Bulge.

The museum in Blois, though small, is of particular

interest to me personally, and has special interest for British tourists as the area was of particular importance for the parachutings of agents from England during the Occupation. Museums in the north of France, though not dedicated exclusively to war displays, usually have war sections in them. This is true for Toul, for example. In areas around Dombasle, in Lorraine, there are roadside markers commemorating where Resistance fighters met their death, and occasionally, there are markers for American soldiers who met their end near that particular spot.

Consequently, any listing is of necessity incomplete. Those museums and places below are ones I know. The reader may well add ones of his or her own. I list them alphabetically.

ALENÇON: MUSÉE LECLERC. Tourist office in Alençon. The Free French forces, from the Occupation to the Liberation.

ARROMANCHES: MUSÉE DU DÉBARQUEMENT. Place du 6 juin. Museum and film about the artificial port set up by the British forces on D+1.

AVRANCHES: MUSÉE DE LA SECONDE GUERRE MONDIAL. Just south of Avranches on the National Highway. Concentrates on D-Day and fighting in and around the Cotentin Peninsula. The Saint James war cemetery is 12 miles south of Avranches. The impressive Monument to Patton, now American territory, with soil and trees brought from the USA, stands on Place Patton.

BAYEUX: MUSÉE MÉMORIAL DE LA BATAILLE DE NORMANDIE. Contains a chronological and detailed presentation of the Battle of Normandy, divided into

British Zone and American Zone displays. Omaha Beach is easily accessed from Bayeux.

BÉNOUVILLE: PEGASUS BRIDGE and the MUSÉE DES TROUPES AÉROPORTÉES. Of particular interest for the veterans of the 6th Airborne Division. Complete with the bagpipes of Bill Millin.

BLOIS: MUSÉE DE LA RÉSISTANCE, DE LA DÉPORTATION ET DE LA LIBÉRATION. The French Resistance displays are of particular interest.

CAEN: MEMORIAL: UN MUSÉE POUR LA PAIX. From World War I to the present, including a section on Nobel Prize winners for peace. Elaborate displays from both wars.

CHERBOURG: MUSÉE DE LA GUERRE ET DE LA LIBÉRATION. Situated high above the city and the sea, the museum, in addition to its many displays, affords a splendid view of the harbor from which many Americans set sail for home.

L'AIGLE: MUSÉE JUIN 44. Historical scenes from 1940 to 1944, presented by the BBC.

OUISTREHAM: MUSÉE DU MUR DE L'ATLANTIQUE and the MUSÉE DE No 4 COMMANDO. Two museums concerning the debarkation on Sword Beach on D-Day.

POINTE DU HOC: a spectacular site, a promontory high above the sea, Le Hoc Point, taken by United States Rangers with heavy loss of life. The site is as close to the feel of a battle site as one can get, with craters of bombs still as they were in 1944.

PORT-EN-BASSIN: MUSÉE DES ÉPAVES SOUS-MARINES DU DÉBARQUEMENT. Remains of craft sunk off the coast of this small fishing town during the D-Day invasion.

SAINTE-MÈRE-ÉGLISE: MUSÉE DES TROUPES AÉROPORTÉES. A center of American parachute landings on the night of June 5–6, 1944, this museum commemorates that night.

STE-MARIE-DU-MONT: MUSÉE DU DÉBARQUEMENT. A museum installed in a German bunker, with particular emphasis on the American landings at Utah Beach, where there is now a small but interesting museum, complete with landing craft and Sherman tank. Nearby is the first of the so-called Bornes de la Liberté that go as far as Bastogne in Belgium, the road markers tracing the route of Liberation of France by Patton's Third Army.

QUINÉVILLE: MUSÉE DE LA LIBÉRTÉ. The museum presents a historical evocation of the Second World War, including dioramas and posters.